THE
LEADERS
COMPETENCIES

Dr. Gregory L. Cruell

ISBN: 978-1-4834-4626-4 (sc)
ISBN: 978-1-4834-4625-7 (e)

Because of the dynamic nature of the Internet, any web addresses or
links contained in this book may have changed since publication and
may no longer be valid. The views expressed in this work are solely those
of the author and do not necessarily reflect the views of the publisher,
and the publisher hereby disclaims any responsibility for them.

Any people depicted in stock imagery provided by Thinkstock are
models, and such images are being used for illustrative purposes only.
Certain stock imagery © Thinkstock.

Lulu Publishing Services rev. date: 03/08/2016

ACKNOWLEDGEMENTS

I would like to thank all of the leaders and laborers, both past and present, with whom I have served, and who have lived the principles of this book in conduct and deed. Their influence has made a difference in my life and the development of the Ethnos Leadership process. I am grateful for the relationships that we share because *"without relationship, there is no leadership."*

To my precious wife for life and best friend, Deirdre, who has been as Barnabas was to Paul, my God-sent encourager: Your love and support have made me a better leader. Thank you.

To my children, Nicole, Stephanie, and Genese, you have been created to make a difference in the world. Always remember that you are all Ethnos Leaders.

To the reader, it is our sincere desire at Ethnos Leadership that in these pages, you will discover additional tools and truths that will assist you in a lifetime leadership journey that will make a difference in the world.

"There is no final race. There is no finish line. The competent leader just keeps running."

G. L. Cruell

CONTENTS

THE WHAT AND WHY OF ETHNOS LEADERSHIP

Leadership and mentorship are the opposite sides of the same coin. For leadership to be authentic, there must be mentorship. You cannot have one without the other. Our philosophy concerning this concept is seen in what we call the Ethnos Equation:

Mentorship: Purposeful Relationships + Authentic Accountability = Professional Responsibility

Mentorship Diagram

The *Merriam-Webster Dictionary* defines a professional or professionalism as *"the conduct, aims, or qualities that characterize or mark a particular profession."* This definition implies that professionalism encompasses a number of different attributes, and together these attributes identify and define a professional.

Mentorship is the non-negotiable epicenter of Ethnos Leadership. Mentorship in Ethnos Leadership is the *professional responsibility* that is acquired and required for organizational health and well-being.

At every level in the organization, the leader and the followers need a mentor for *accountability*. Purposeful relationships are valued, trusted, and respected. Bonds or alliances of this manner open the door to forthright accountability. Being accountable or answerable to a trusted friend, advisor, or mentor provides both protection and correction through life and leadership in an environment that is safe because it is trusted and valued. Responsibility simply means cultivating one's ability to respond to the distinct circumstances and situations of one's personal and organizational leadership influence via the Ethnos Leadership process (*Discover, Develop, Disciple, Make A Difference*).

The leader's *professional responsibility* is learned and acquired through the evolution of intentional *mentorship* by virtue of *purposeful relationships*. Purposeful relationships are rooted in the principle attributed to Saint Francis of Assisi, *"seek first to understand rather than to be understood."* An understanding of the organization's goals and the people or team that make the organization go and grow are informed by this basic universal principle.

The word "nations" in the original Greek is *"ethnos."* Ethnos maybe defined as *"a group of people bound together by the same customs, conduct, language, behaviors or other distinguishing features."* There are 3 modules in the Ethnos Leadership Process: *character, capabilities and competencies.* Each module has 4 sessions.

At the conclusion of each individual session, participants will create a summary of the principles they have discovered and that they have decided to develop. This aspect of the Ethnos Leadership process is the *Personal Leadership Perspective* (PLP). During week 14, participants will combine their 12 Personal Leadership Perspective summaries to create a cumulative plan or writing of the *Personal Leaders Character Story* (PLCS) that initiates Phase V of the process entitled: *"Commitment to Investing in Personal and Organizational Transformation."*

The Ethnos Leadership Process is designed to be completed in 14 weeks. The emphasis is on a platform of *self-evaluation* and *self-reflection.* The conclusion of the process is a commitment to a lifetime of *discovering, developing,* and *discipling* (mentoring) of those that we lead who are bound together by the Ethnos Leadership process and making a *difference* across *"nations"* (*ethnos*– people's lives).

To a person who has been leading for many years, or to a person who is just beginning the leadership journey, Ethnos Leadership is a blueprint to reinforce, strengthen, and sharpen present or existing leadership skills by expanding one's perspective of leadership.

This book contains the 4 sessions of the competencies module, or *"The Investment is Worth It."* Competence is the proven abilities and improved capabilities of the leader. It is the capacity to function in one's profession successfully and efficiently.

Competence includes a combination of knowledge, basic requirements or capabilities, abilities, behavior, and attitude. The competent leader in any organization understands the responsibility to mentor others. The competent leader is on a never-ending quest of proficiency and mastery of his or her profession for the sake of mentoring others. The aim of this quest is to *discover, develop, disciple* (mentor) to make a *difference* in the lives of others who makes a difference in our world. This is Ethnos Leadership.

"The quality of a person's life is in direct proportion to their commitment to excellence and competence, regardless of their chosen field of endeavor."
Adapted from Vince Lombardi

For more information about the Ethnos Leadership Process contact us at: ethnosleadership@gmail.com

Session I

Mentorship in Leadership: The Non-Negotiable

Foundation

"A mentor is someone whose hindsight can become your foresight."

Anonymous

In the mid-1970s, corporate America redefined mentoring as a career development strategy. A strong foundation of organizational mentoring is needed to build and retain a healthy workforce that can react quickly to change and can develop, adapt, and regenerate itself over time.[1] The passing of the torch of leadership is a constant reality. When retirement arrives for senior leaders, a solid functional mentoring

---

[1] http://www.educause.edu/research-publications/books/cultivating-careers-professional-development-campus-it/chapter-5-importance-mentors. Accessed March 20, 2015.

program helps to ensure the continuity of established standards and goals that have shaped the company's success. Mentoring is one of the oldest forms of influence and knowledge sharing. Its origins can be traced to the days of the Ancient Greeks with Mentor, who was Odysseus's trusted counselor and advisor. A mentor is an individual—usually older, but always more experienced—who helps and guides another individual's development.

A study of successful personalities and leaders throughout the course of history reveals that most men and women had mentors who cared about their growth and development. Alexander the Great had Aristotle; King Arthur of England had Merlin; Paul of Tarsus of the first century mentored Timothy who later became a Bishop; the poet T. S. Eliot had Ezra Pound; Dr. Martin Luther King Jr. had Dr. Benjamin Elijah Mays; Beethoven and Mozart had Haydn; Helen Keller had Anne Sullivan; and Oprah Winfrey had Barbara Walters. The list is endless.[2]

Mary Abbajay a partner in the Careerstone Group, a professional consulting company, says, *"Being a good mentor requires more than just experience. It requires a willingness to reflect and share one's own experiences, including one's failures.*[3] Mentors need to share both their *"how to do it right"* and their *"how I did it wrong* "stories. Transparency and honesty of this caliber provide valuable opportunities for learning. This will

[2] http://www.brighthub.com/office/human-resources/articles
[3] IBID. Accessed March 19, 2015.

involve commitment, time, and energy to devote to the mentoring relationship.

Management and leadership expert Peter Drucker once stated, *"There can be no genuine success without a successor."*[4] To build a successful business empire is one thing, but for it to live on past one's own time is another.

With this thought in mind, the perspective of this session is that mentorship and leadership are the opposite sides of the same coin. It cannot be negotiated but must be promulgated. In business, there is an existing principle that says, *"Everything is negotiable."* This principle may be true when the conversation concerns goods, services, or products. The ability to negotiate a better price or a greater discount without comprising quality for one's organization is a must in the business world. However, the thesis of this session is that mentorship is not about a product or services per say; mentorship is about people.

People are a company's or an organization's most valuable asset. Therefore, mentorship must never be *negotiated*, but must be *perpetuated*. Mentorship is a non-negotiable standard for any and every organization that desires perpetual success. To negotiate is to deal or bargain with another concerning a particular matter. A bargain is seen as an advantageous acquisition at a less than usual cost; an agreement between parties.[5]

[4] http://exchange2011.s3.amazonaws.com/LeavingLegacy_Article.pdf. Accessed March 17, 2015.
[5] www.dictionary.com. Accessed March 18, 2015.

There is no bargain price for success. There is no bartering involved in mentoring. It is a *non-negotiable standard* that must be in place and functional for present and future success.

The competent leader recognizes that mentorship in leadership cannot be legislated or be a mandatory requirement within an organization.

It must be a matter of choice. Both the mentor and mentee have to believe that the ensuing relationship "fits." If one's shoe size is 8 or 9, to ask a member of the team (mentor or mentee) to wear a size 12 is simply not going to work or be comfortable. In the establishment of this mutual union of development, there are elements of both personal and professional investments involved. When we think about the largest investment that one may make in life, it normally involves the purchase of a home.

It does not matter if it is a 30-year mortgage or 15-year mortgage, it is the price that we are willing to pay to own our home. Prior to investing in a particular home, there are particular elements that also apply in a mentor/mentee relationship. Perhaps the two most important elements are *time* and *money*. This means the time that it takes to find the right home and then ultimately the final cost of the home. It is an investment. Statesman and scientist Benjamin Franklin in his letter entitled, *"Advice to a Young Tradesman, Written by An Old One,"* says to his friend A. B.; *"As you have desired it of me, I write the following hints, which have been of service to me, and may, if observed, be so to you. Remember that time is money….*"[6] The essence of this metaphor is that good business people, who want to stay in business, do not squander opportunities and money.

The time that leaders invest *"is the currency"* (money) that, at some point, produces compound interest in the lives of those who they choose to mentor.

Cal Ripken Jr., is baseball's all-time Iron Man. He retired from baseball in 2001 after 21 seasons with the Baltimore Orioles. In 1995, Ripken broke Lou Gehrig's record for consecutive games played (2,130) and ended his streak in 1998 after playing 2,632 consecutive games. On one occasion during an interview, Ripken stated, *"The value of a mentor…I don't know what value you can place on it, but the right words spoken at the right time from a person that's been through it before, can make all the difference…."*[7]

Oprah Winfrey is without question one of the world's most well-known and celebrated personalities. She has inspired millions with her television show, magazines, movies, and humanitarian efforts. But Oprah wasn't always the strong woman she is today. As a child, she was very insecure but found strength in her fourth-grade teacher, Mary Duncan. Duncan often stayed after school with Winfrey on a regular basis, taking her under her wing and asking her to help out with classroom tasks. *"She helped me choose*

---

[6] http://quotes.yourdictionary.com/articles/who-said-remeber-that-time-is-money. Accessed March 18, 2015.
[7] http://www.hsph.harvard.edu/chc/wmy/Celebrities/cal_ripken. Accessed March 18, 2015.

books and let me help her grade papers," recalls Winfrey, stressing the importance of their relationship:

"A mentor is someone who allows you to see the hope inside yourself. A mentor is someone who allows you to know that no matter how dark the night, in the morning joy will come. A mentor is someone who allows you to see the higher part of yourself when sometimes it becomes hidden to your own view. I don't think anybody makes it in the world without some form of mentorship. And we are all mentors to people, even when we don't know it." [8]

Why Do We Need Mentors?

"The reasonable thing is to learn from those who can teach."
Sophocles

In their book, *"The Elements of Mentoring,"* Brad Johnson and Charles Ridley offer their readers a concise, clear summary of the fundamental principles of mentoring. The aim of their book was to get to the *"nuts and bolts of being a good mentor."* [9]

If the ancient philosopher Sophocles is correct, the reason why we need mentors is that there are still some things that we need to learn, and we need those who are capable of teaching to teach us those lessons! Throughout our life's journey, most of us will

---

[8] http://www.degreescout.com/blog/inspiring-the-inspired-7-mentors-of-great-historical-figures. Accessed March 18, 2015.
[9] Johnson, Brad W. and Ridley, Charles R. The Elements of Mentoring. (New York: Palgrave Macmillan), 2004, xvi.

recall what we learned from our parents, teachers, professors, coaches, and others from whom we learned very valuable lessons about life.

For the seasoned leader, and even the new leader, one very valuable lesson that most of us have learned in our life experiences thus far is that there is *always more to learn!* After graduation from high school, college, graduate studies, postgraduate studies; 15, 20, or 30 years in the workplace environment... *what life has taught us is that there's always more to learn!* Effectiveness in leadership will always call for consistent and persistent growth and learning.

This type of leader always looks to determine the *"pulse"* of the environment to which he/she belongs and asks how do I, as a leader help, the organization to be alive and thrive in our community. Never being afraid to ask themselves the question, *"What do I still need to learn to be a significant contributor to the success of our organization?"* Enter the mentor.

PART I: CREATING A CULTURE OF MENTORING

. . . .

"Mentorship is about learning and growing from relationships that matter."

G. L. Cruell

Learning is the fundamental aim and primary purpose of mentoring. One reason that mentoring relationships fail is that the learning process is not tended to and the focus on learning is not maintained.[10]

Lois Zachary states that in order to maximize the relationship between mentor and mentee, the mentor must continue to grow and develop. This type of partnership and relationship begins with self-learning that underscores the reality and necessity of self-leadership. If you cannot lead self, you will most likely not be able to lead anyone else. Zachary further states, *"Without a mentor's commitment to personal learning, the potential effectiveness of the learning relationship is greatly reduced.*

In the preface of *The Mentor's Guide,* Zachary encourages mentors to *"reach out, keep reaching out, and keep bringing in. It will enable you to reap an enduring harvest."*[11] The metaphor and principle that Zachary shares is very powerful and clear. *"Whatever you sow*

---

[10] Zachary, Lois. *The Mentor's Guide: Facilitating Effective Learning Relationships.* (San Francisco: Jossey-Bass), 2000, 1.

[11] IBID, xxi.

(plant) in others is what you will also reap and receive from others." For those who invest in mentoring others are the mark of a personal investment both in persons and for the organization to which they belong.

Leadership is about being trusted to lead. It is often been said that an organization's most valuable assets are its people. There is no statement that is more true and needed to be recognized than this. It is understood and recognized that in any administration of any organization, there will always be paperwork that is needed to accomplish the task. Yet when we focus on *"people-work"* the *"paperwork"* or administrative responsibilities will follow naturally.

When team members or employees believe that they are important to an organization, it is without question they will always go the extra mile. When there is a belief that they are valued and important employees, they will approach their daily assignments from the perspective of dependability and reliability. This was initiated by the organizational leadership's expressions of the value of every team member.

Mentorship is about making the investment in *"people-work"* to *"pass the baton"* of learning and teaching what we as leaders have been taught. It is an investment in the future that will produce a harvest of guaranteed success. The practice of mentoring or passing the baton has evolved to the point where traditional one-to-one mentoring is only one approach to this concept.

We must use every form of mentoring available to pass the baton. Peer-to-peer mentoring and team mentoring are becoming more commonplace in many organizations. How do we accomplish the end-state of mentoring? Face-to-face and distance mentoring are two very successful methods. Distance mentoring has grown to such mediums as videoconferencing, email, FaceTime, etc. In other words, technology has boosted our capabilities to create and practice a mentoring culture.[12] Elements of a mentoring culture include:

- The ability to listen and learn
- Being driven and dedicated to the process
- Being a good partner in the relationship

A proven ability to *listen* and *learn* is an important aspect of a mentoring culture because of the investment of time and resources. The competent leader understands the value of mentoring and yet is not willing to waste time or resources simply for the sake of a "casual" mentoring opportunity.

Identifying within the organization those team members who are *driven* and *dedicated* to learning and growing is where the competent leader makes his or her investment. There is an anticipation and enthusiasm that creates an excitement in every meeting with one's mentor. It is not forced or legislated. It is a contribution of one's self to the entire process and pursuit of growth and development. This type

---

[12] IBID, xxiii.

of individual drive is dedicated to and possesses a "whatever it takes mentality."

What this means is the cost of the process. Whatever it takes, I want and need what my mentor is willing to provide. It is *being a good partner* in the process. A process is a series of actions or steps taken in order to achieve a particular end. In other words, what is expected in this partnership? A partner does his or her part!

The mentor's role is to *impart*, while the mentee's role is not to *depart* the process. Within a mentoring culture and relationship, begin with the end of the process in mind.

Ask questions: *"What do I expect from this mentoring relationship?" "How long is this mentoring relationship going to last?" "Should I look for other mentors within the organization?" "Am I getting what I need for my personal aspirations and development in this mentoring relationship?"* A mentoring culture helps to answer these questions by the resilience of an organization. If a mentoring program is not sufficiently embedded in a supportive organizational culture that values learning and development, it rarely flourishes.

An intentional framework of mentoring is to create a workable process and solution for developing competent leaders for the future. It is certainly not an easy task or assignment for an organization. Yet with persistent and steadfast effort in the process of creating and establishing a culture of mentoring the rewards and benefits to the organization will prove that the effort and investment were worth it.

PART II: THE NON-NEGOTIABLE OF ENCOURAGEMENT IN MENTORING

"The spirited horse, which will try to win the race of its own accord, will run even faster if encouraged."

Publius Ovidius Naso Ovid

According to the *New World Encyclopedia*, Rudolf Dreikurs was an American psychiatrist and educator who developed Alfred Adler's system of *"individual psychology"* into a pragmatic method for understanding the purposes of misbehavior in children and for stimulating cooperative behavior without punishment or reward. Adler and Dreikurs firmly believed that encouragement was essential to improvement of behavior and human relationships.[13]

Adler and Dreikurs believed that behavior is a result of a search for significance within a social setting. Dreikurs said, *"Anticipation influences outcome—the fear of making a mistake leads to mistakes. Anyone who can alter the expectations of people can change their behavior."* Thereby encouragement and positive support have a direct correlation with improved behavior in others.

As a leading proponent of the power of encouragement, Dreikurs taught, *"A child needs encouragement as a plant needs water."* In other words, encouragement is essential. Children (and adults)

---

[13] http://www.newworldencyclopedia.org/entry/Rudolf_Dreikurs. Accessed March 28, 2015.

may not die without encouragement, but they will certainly wither.[14] Mentoring is a structured and trusting relationship that brings people together for the purpose of guidance, support, and encouragement aimed at developing the competence, and character of the mentee.

From Dreikurs' perspective, regardless of age, encouragement is the ability that helps bring people together under the banner of *courage added*. These types of relationships are supportive in nature and assist the process of developing people into who they want to be: To discover and know that they are capable and resilient, to be able to enjoy life, and, as Dreikurs stated, *"To have the courage to be imperfect, to feel free to make mistakes and to learn from them."*[15]

Encouragement from a mentor to a mentee, may sometimes take on the persona or personality of Walter D. Wintle's poem "I Think I Can."

> *"If you think you are beaten, you are.*
> *If you think you dare not, you don't!*
> *If you want to win, but think you can't,*
> *It's almost certain you won't.*
>
> *If you think you'll lose, you're lost. For out in the*
> *world we find success begins with a fellow's will;*
> *It's all in the state of the mind.*

---

[14] IBID, Accessed March 28, 2015.

[15] http://blog.positivediscipline.com/2009/09/encouragement-what-does-it-mean-and-how.html. Accessed March 28, 2015.

Life's battles don't always go
To the stronger and faster man,
But sooner or later the one who wins
Is the man or woman who thinks they can."[16]

Due to a mentor's own experiences in life, addressing discouragement as a leader is essential. A genuine mentor recognizes and acknowledges the fact that some matters can become so challenging and difficult that discouragement rather than encouragement shows up for work! The wise mentor remembers and understands that there will be times, if not now, then sooner or later, when the mentee perhaps contemplates quitting because of discouragement. Proverbs 25:11 says, *"A word spoken at the right time is like gold apples on a silver tray."*

Joseph Joubert once stated, *"In the commerce of speech, use only coin of gold and silver."* Rudyard Kipling said, *"Words are the most powerful drug used by mankind."* The right words spoken at the right time releases the influence of encouragement even in the midst of discouragement.

Researchers at the University of Arizona used digital voice recorders over an eight-year period to study how many words hundreds of American and Mexican college students spoke over several days. The students carried the voice-activated recorders for almost all of their waking hours, on average about

---

[16] http://www.bizmove.com/inspiration/m9b.htm. Accessed November 28, 2015.

17 hours a day. The study found that women spoke 16,215 words a day, while men spoke 15,669.[17] The study suggests that during the course of our day, there a lot of words that are spoken and exchanged. Some words carry great significance, while others carried very little significance. It has been said, *"Some people have to say something, while others really have something to say."* Encouragement always has something to say. In preparation for the mentor and mentee session, the mentor has prepared to really have something of significance to say.

Let the words that we exchange, both mentor and mentee, be of such significance and mutual benefit that those words become the foundation of encouragement that ultimately adds courage for our collective leadership journey that is non-negotiable.

---

[17] http://abcnews.go.com/Technology/story?id=3348076. Accessed March 28, 2015.

Part III: The Non-Negotiable of Aspiration in Mentoring

"Example is not the main thing in influencing others, it's the only thing."

Albert Schweitzer

The *Online Etymology Dictionary* says that aspiration is the *"action of breathing into,"* from the Latin, *"aspirationem."* Our English definition of aspiration is a *"hope or ambition of achieving something; a steadfast longing for a higher goal, an earnest desire for something above one."* To aspire is *"to climb up to, to endeavor to obtain."*[18]

Some leaders actively and determinedly seek out their leadership role in their professional or personal life. For others, their leadership role is cast upon them. Either way, once you take on the position of leadership in whatever circumstance, you need to choose carefully how you frame, or view, what leadership means to you. The aspirational mentor is determined to be in a better position to positively influence the lives of others. This is the fundamental mindset of an aspirational leader. They see their leadership as a privilege and not just a position, and in this position, their aim, goal, and desire is to mentor.

---

[18] http://www.oxforddictionaries.com/. Accessed March 30, 2015.

An aspirational leader and mentor is someone who intentionally focuses on positively influencing the capacity and the competency of their people to flourish in their professional and personal lives and to strive to perform at their best.

Aspirational leadership is a choice, and while there are many contributing factors to success in any leadership role, an aspirational leader is someone who genuinely views leadership as a privilege and not just a role. They value relationships, model good character and integrity, and firmly place trust of self and with others at the center of their decision-making and actions. An aspirational mentor emphasizes in deed and conduct the qualities and values of life that are needed to sustain aspirations.

The aspirational mentor exemplifies and provides a setting for the survival of the aspirations a mentee possesses that created or initiated the relationship in the first place. Aspirations are more intangible because they are not necessarily solidified by goals or objectives. Aspirations are currents of internal desire—they are seldom more concrete than that.[19] Aspirational mentors help mentees to take ownership of their own development because of the internal passion to succeed and achieve more in their chosen profession. The International Mentoring Association says, *"Aspirations are feelings and attitudes that pulsate outward and do not have a validated, approved, recognized,*

---

[19] http://mentoringassociation.org/connect/mentors-and-leaders-aspirations/. Accessed March 30, 2015.

or even articulate object." There is no guarantee that anything can happen as a result of these aspirations.

The mentor's role is to help the mentee to translate aspirations into organizational goals while not losing sight of the generative, aspirational vitality that lies behind them. In so doing, the aspirational mentor supports the mentee's need for openness, perceptiveness, flexibility, and enthusiasm as he or she engages in pursuing organizational goals of bringing to others new products, new services, and new relationships that promise more expansive and more encompassing ways of living. The aspirational mentor's role is as bold as it is complex.

The aim of the aspirational mentor is to help the mentee to see and articulate his or her aspirations, to envision how to realize them, and then, through thick and thin, help their mentee to keep his or her aspirations alive. The intent of the aspirational mentor is to develop the type of relationships where leadership and mentorship become synonymous, valued, and purposely pursued. When this is accomplished, the end result will produce not only new aspirations, but inspiration within the organization because the hope to achieve higher goals is active and alive in the aspirational mentor and everybody knows it.

PART IV: THE NON-NEGOTIABLE OF MOTIVATION IN MENTORING

··

*"Inspiration and motivation are the **DNA** (Do Not Abandon) of leadership."*

G. L. Cruell

The *Oxford English Dictionary* provides a foundational definition of motivation from the Late Latin *"motivus,"* and *"movere,"* which means *"to move."*

It further means at its core, *"a motive or reason for doing something with enthusiasm."* Enthusiasm from its Late Latin origins from the Greek *"enthousiasmos,"* and its root word *"enthous"* means *"possessed by a god, inspired."* Motivation therefore becomes a desire or willingness to do or move with enthusiasm.

From this perspective, a mentor is a motivator, one who provides a motive or motives and provokes or causes someone *"to move with enthusiasm."* If the idea in a mentor-mentee relationship is to cause one to move, the question becomes where are we going? Which direction or path should the mentor-mentee relationship move towards with enthusiasm?

The Holden Leadership Center at the University of Oregon in an article entitled "Motivating Your Members" states, *"Fostering motivation within an organization first begins by helping the group members* to develop a good healthy image of self."[20] Creating this healthy self-image within an organization is based upon five basic rules for leaders and mentors to exemplify:

- Do what's right
- Do the best you can
- Treat others as you'd like to be treated
- Exhibit a positive attitude
- Expect the best at all times[21]

From this vantage point, a mentor will motivate a mentee by establishing a consistent reputation for *"doing what is right."* Doing what is right is the leadership attribute of integrity. Doing the best that you can is a persistent pursuit of one's best efforts. It can never be a pursuit of perfection simply because no one is perfect. However, Vince Lombardi legendary coach of the Green Bay Packers once said, *"that if you pursue perfection, you will catch excellence."* A mentee is not looking for a perfect mentor; it is the excellence of conduct and behavior that is sought after.

"Treating others as you would like to be treated" is conduct that gives dignity and respect to all and not to just a select few. *"Exhibiting a positive attitude"* is a trait that is developed and persistently seen even in the face of things that sometimes seem to be too hard

---

20 http://leadership.uoregon.edu/resources/exercises_tips/skills/ motivating_your_members. Accessed March 29, 2015.
[21] IBID, March 29, 2015.

to do, understand, or overcome. It is a statement by one's life and actions that exudes hope that everything is going to work out. *"Expecting the best at all times"* of team members or employees provides an atmosphere of confidence that when practiced, will push the organization to greater productivity. People simply produce more when their leaders believe and expect the best at all times. The external motivators from the organizational leadership feed the internal personal motivators.

Continual stimuli for personal and organizational motivation may also be seen in *L.I.F.E.*

- Loyal
- Invested
- Focus
- Energy

Loyalty is simply a strong sense of support and allegiance. When a team member or employee experiences this aspect of *L.I.F.E.* from the organization, a sense of security and safety comes in the same package. When the competent leader is *invested*, a purposeful mentoring is ongoing. An investor's resources (time, money, material) are extremely valuable and because this is clearly understood, and an ROI (return on investment) at some point in the future is anticipated and expected. *Focus* may be defined as the center of interest or attention. In many organizations, leaders expect employees or team members to be focused on the company's interests. However, when the organization's center of interest is on its team members or employees, leaders can *"expect the best at all times."*

The bonds of *L.I.F.E.* in this type of work environment when purposefully practiced and appreciated organizationally become energizing. *Energy* adds excitement that compels and inspires one to move or act. An organization of this nature is an anomaly that when revealed to others becomes an example of a championship mindset.

When competent leaders determine that *L.I.F.E.* is worth living, a strategy for creating and implementing *L.I.F.E.* will emerge. Most of us, if not all of us, can recall those moments in when a significant accomplishment or achievement was finalized and our overwhelming sense of satisfaction or enjoyment of that moment.

Responsible, competent leaders build upon those moments because of the motivation that is provided. Public recognition or affirmation is also a tremendous motivator of incalculable value that most people will never verbalize. Yet when it is given, this external motivator does more for a person sometimes than a monetary bonus. Money is not everything for everyone, and sometimes public recognition of a task or a job well done provides reward enough intrinsically for the next task.

To further undergird motivation, Bernard Bass puts forth one of four components of transformational leadership that he calls *"inspirational motivation."* The aim of transformational leadership is, as the name suggests, to transform. If it is true that no leader can motivate a team member or follower, what Bass suggests is that motivation comes through inspiration imparted by others.

In his book *"Transformational Leadership,"* Bass defines and describes inspirational motivation as *"the degree to which the leader articulates a vision that is appealing and inspiring to followers. Leaders with inspirational motivation challenge followers by exemplifying high standards, constantly and consistently communicating optimism about future goals, and providing meaning for the task at hand."*[22]

In the application of inspirational motivation, transformational leaders need to provide by example a strong sense of purpose if team members are to be motivated to act. Purpose and meaning provide the energy that drives a group forward. The visionary aspects of this type of leadership are supported by communication skills that make the vision understandable, precise, powerful, and engaging. Team members are willing to invest more effort in their tasks, they are encouraged and optimistic about the future, and they believe in their abilities and the abilities of the leader who inspired and motivated them. [23] Motivation is likened unto the story of "The

---

[22] Bass, Bernard. Transformational Leadership: Industrial, Military and Educational Impact. (Mahwah: Lawrence Erlbaum Associates Publishers, 1998), 5.
[23] IBID, 5.

Essence of Survival: *"Every morning on the African plain a gazelle wakes up. It knows it must run faster than the fastest lion or it will be killed. Every morning on the African plain a lion wakes up. It knows it must outrun the slowest gazelle or it will starve to death. The moral of the story is it doesn't matter whether you are the lion or the gazelle, when the sun comes up, you'd better be running."*[24] Do Not Abandon (DNA) motivation; it will help you and those who you lead to survive.

---

[24] Montano, Dan. Economist Newspaper Ltd., London. "The other dimension: Technology and the City of London: A survey", "Lions or gazelles?", p. 37, July 6, 1985.

PART V: THE NON-NEGOTIABLE OF PERSONAL GROWTH IN MENTORING

According to *The Odyssey,* Mentor was entrusted with the education and development of Odysseus's young son, Telemachus. Mentor was the consummate teacher, who faithfully educated Telemachus in the ways of the world and gave him the required knowledge to live in the world. When Telemachus grew up and Odysseus returned, his responsibilities as mentor were complete. Although the original concept of a mentor still exists today, it is not the same as it was in the *Odyssey.*[25]

Today's mentor is a partner in an evolving learning relationship focused on the goals and objectives of the mentee.

In this learning relationship, although the central idea is for the mentee to learn, on the other side of the coin, what is the mentor learning?

When considering the popular phrase that *"leadership is not a destination, but a journey,"* the question that must be asked is where does the mentor find him or herself on the path of growing for the purpose of instructing? If we all agree that because we are competent leaders and we have not arrived at a final destination of our leadership, what then is our

---

[25] Zachary, Lois. The Mentor's Guide: Facilitating Effective Learning Relationships. (San Francisco: Jossey Bass Publishers), 2000, p. 161.

mindset for continual growth as a leader? Personal growth as a leader mentor becomes a necessary part of our leadership journey when we acknowledge the fact that none of us have arrived at our final destination of learning.

A mentor's own growth and development are nurtured by renewal, reflection, and realignment. To renew is *"to replenish, to revive or reestablish. To restore to a former state as if new again."* A reflection is that *"which is seen or an idea that is expressed."* To realign is to line up again with the priorities and the urgency of mentorship. This principle or truth of urgency for realigning or lining up with mentoring is seen in the mission of the *"Be A Mentor Program"* in California. A page on the organizations website states, *"Youth are in desperate need of a mentor, someone that they can talk to, spend time with, and who will be their friend. They need someone to say "I believe in YOU!" The time a mentor spends with the youth can be spent focusing on schoolwork, exploring goals for the future, going to movies or other events, or simply talking and listening. You are only asked to spend 4 to 6 hours per month together. The personal rewards for both the mentor and the mentee are endless."*[26]

The *"Be A Mentor Program"* founded in 1992 has as its top and only priority the youth of the community. The concept is the same in whatever community we are a part of, whether it's in the military community, the business community, the local YMCA or our

[26] http://www.volunteermatch.org/search/opp173855.jsp. Accessed April 3, 2015.

community at home with our sons and daughters. To be a mentor is simply those who are *"senior in experience"* making an investment in the lives of those who are *"junior to them in experience"* that makes a perpetual difference. Winston Churchill once stated, *"We make a living by what we get; we make a life by what we give."* Mentorship is not necessarily about what *we get* in the relationship we have with our mentee. It is more about what *we give.*

To renew or restore as new again, is recapturing and regaining the perspective of the purpose of mentor-mentee partnership. A partner does his or her part. The mentor's part is to *impart* as Mentor did with Telemachus. The dialogue of this partnership triggers a sense of urgency and preparedness for any and all sessions. To renew or to be restored as new again ought to produce for the mentor an intellectual and emotional stimulation centered in the fact that my mentee is depending on me.

My part as a mentor is to make a difference that will last a lifetime in my mentee's leadership development.

Lois Zachary states, *"Critically reflective mentors are more focused in their mentorship relationships simply due to the investment."* Reflective mentors recognize that their investment in the mentor-mentee relationship carries over to their personal and professional relationships as the benefits and habits of reflection become internalized. [27] To be in position of leadership

---

[27] Zachary, Lois p.162.

over any period of time just by the wear and tear of everyday responsibilities brings us to this place for the need of renewal, reflection, and realignment or the need for continued personal growth.

Dr. Bruce Johnson, in an article entitled *"What Does it Mean to Experience Personal Growth?,"* states that experiencing true personal and professional growth is really about cultivating conditions. It includes a mindset and an attitude that is necessary to support changes in your life and your career.[28] The idea of growing personally or professionally is usually born out of a desire to do more, become more, or adapt to changes within your life that were either expected or unexpected. Any type of growth requires both a willingness to look past and look beyond.

If you look only at the past, you may allow questions, regrets, or any other conditions you've associated with those events to become the dominant thought and stall the initial steps towards growth. [29] Personal growth includes the capability to make decisions to discard thoughts, habits, and beliefs that do not serve you well. We always have a choice regarding the thoughts that we focus on. It is not an easy process at times when you become accustomed to patterns of thought that maintain the status quo, especially if you have developed comfortable routines for your life and

---

[28] http://www.affordablequalitywriting.com/blog/2013/08/what-does-it-mean-experience-personal-growth#.VR0nA_nF-Sp. Accessed April 2, 2015.

[29] IBID. Accessed April 2, 2015.

career. Personal and professional growth does not mean that you have to completely change; rather, it encourages you to learn and expand upon what you are capable of doing.[30]

Cultivating a mindset or condition for allowing personal and professional growth to occur does not mean waiting for an opportunity for growth, but making yourself *opportunity-ready*. Comedian Milton Berle once said, *"If opportunity does not knock, build a door."* It is learning to become *proactive* instead of *reactive* as a mentor by the development of an attitude that will allow you to grow without waiting for circumstances or conditions that force you to change. Growth is an ongoing process, a constant evolution that as a mentor you never give up on reaching your full potential.

Believe in yourself, be ready for change, take proactive steps to learn, and start growing from within. *"An eagle perched on a branch is never afraid of the branch breaking. Its trust is not in the branch, but in its own wings. Always believe in yourself"* Anonymous.

Cultivating an intrinsic state of mind and a devotion for personal growth becomes a motivating factor for those that we lead and serve. Those that we lead deserve our best and that simply means cultivating a mindset that says, *"I will be better today than I was yesterday."* Every day is a new opportunity for us to "spread our wings" in personal growth that leads to

---

[30] IBID. Accessed April 2, 2015.

professional growth that produces ineffable benefits in the mentor-mentee relationship. It is this mindset and drive that makes an enduring difference in our organizations and it is non-negotiable.

Summation: Mentorship—
The Non-Negotiable
. . . .

Leadership and mentorship are the opposite sides of the same coin. Mentoring is one of the oldest forms of influence and the sharing of knowledge. Its origins can be traced backed to the days of the Ancient Greeks with Mentor, who was Odysseus's trusted counselor and advisor. A mentor is an individual—usually older, but always more experienced—who helps and guides another individual's development. Essential qualities for an effective mentor include:

- A desire to develop and help others. A good mentor is genuinely interested in helping someone else without a promise of reward.
- Commitment, time, and energy to devote to the mentoring relationship. Current and relevant knowledge, expertise, and/or skills.
- A willingness to share failures and personal experiences. Mentors need to share both their *"how to do it right"* and their *"how I did it wrong"* stories. Both experiences provide valuable opportunities for learning.

Sophocles, an ancient philosopher stated, *"The reasonable thing is to learn from those who can teach."* If Sophocles is correct, the reason why we need mentors is that there is still some things that we need to learn and we need those who are capable of teaching to teach us those lessons!

Throughout our life's journey, most of us will recall what we learned from our parents, teachers, professors, coaches, and others from whom we learned very valuable lessons about life. For the seasoned leader, and even the new leader, one very valuable lesson that most of us have learned in our life and leadership experiences thus far is that there is *always more to learn!*

Lois Zachary concludes that a mentoring culture narrates, growth, development and the resilience of an organization.

If a mentoring program is not sufficiently embedded in a supportive organizational culture that values learning and development, it rarely flourishes. An intentional framework of mentoring as suggested by Zachary's eight hallmarks of mentoring creates a workable process and solution for developing competent leaders for the future.

Mentoring is a structured and trusting relationship that brings people together for the purpose of guidance, support, and encouragement aimed at developing the competence and character of the mentee. Regardless of age, encouragement is the ability that helps bring people together under the banner of *courage added.* These types of relationships are supportive in nature and assist the process of developing people into who they want to be and will become. It has been said,

"Some people have to say something, while others really have something to say."

Encouragement always has something to say. In preparation for the mentor and mentee session, the mentor has prepared to really have something of significance to say. Let the words that we exchange, both mentor and mentee, be of such significance and mutual benefit that those words become the foundation of encouragement.

From the place of encouragement, the mentor-mentee relationship progresses as an ally to aspiration. The International Mentoring Association says *"Aspirations are feelings and attitudes that pulsate outward and do not have a validated, approved, recognized, or even articulate object."* There is no guarantee that anything can happen as a result of these aspirations. The mentor's role is to help the mentee to translate aspirations into organizational goals while not losing sight of the generative, aspirational vitality that lies behind them. The aim of the aspirational mentor is to help the mentee to see and articulate his or her aspirations, to envision how to enact them, and then, through thick and thin, help the mentee to keep his or her aspirations alive.

The alliance of principles of mentorship continues with the strength of motivation. The *Oxford English Dictionary* provides a foundational definition of motivation from the Late Latin *"motivus,"* and *"movere"* which means *"to move."* It further means at its core, *"a motive or reason for doing something with enthusiasm."*

The Holden Leadership Center at the University of Oregon in an article entitled "Motivating Your Members" states, *"Fostering motivation within an organization first begins by helping the group members to develop a good healthy image of self."*[31] Creating this healthy self-image within an organization requires five basic rules for leaders and mentors to exemplify:

- Do what's right
- Do the best you can
- Treat others as you'd like to be treated
- Exhibit a positive attitude
- Expect the best at all times [32]

From this vantage point, a mentor will motivate a mentee by establishing a consistent reputation for *"doing what is right."* Motivation always reveals the goal or object of a person's action. The goal of mentoring is to make both the mentor and mentee better leaders. People simply produce more when their leaders believe and expect the best at all times.

The external motivators from the organizational leadership feed the internal personal motivators. Continual stimuli for personal and organizational motivation may also be seen in *L.I.F.E.*

- Loyal
- Invested

31 http://leadership.uoregon.edu/resources/exercises_tips/skills/motivating_your_members. Accessed March 29, 2015.
[32] IBID, March 29, 2015.

- *Focus*
- *Energy*

According to Bernard Bass, a transformational leader adds to this conversation what he calls *"inspirational motivation."* The aim of transformational leadership is as the name suggests: to transform. Bass suggests that motivation comes through *inspiration* imparted by others. It is a purposeful investment in someone else that breathes and breeds life that provides purpose and meaning concerning the future.

Personal growth as a leader/mentor becomes a necessary part of our leadership journey when we acknowledge the fact that none of us have arrived at our final destination of learning. A mentors' own growth and development are nurtured by renewal, reflection, and realignment.

To renew is *"to replenish, to revive or reestablish. To restore to a former state as if new again."* A reflection is that *"which is seen or an idea that is expressed."* To realign is to line up again with the priorities and the urgency of mentorship. The idea of growing personally or professionally is usually born out of a desire to do more, become more, or adapt to changes within your life that were either expected or unexpected.

Any type of growth requires both a willingness to look past and look beyond. Growth is an ongoing process, a constant evolution that as a leader/mentor you never give up pursuit of because of its ensuing value to the future. With a persistent proactive approach to personal growth, the mature, competent leader fulfills his or her leadership legacy (mentorship). This legacy is fueled and fulfilled through *purposeful relationships* that inspire others to *accountability* that evolves and becomes everyone's *professional responsibility;* which is a dependable means to enduring personal and organizational betterment.

QUESTIONS FOR REFLECTION

1. In many organizations, the strength and validity of mentorship is viewed as having no true meaning. What steps could you take to change this mindset in your organization?

2. In the business world, most would agree that everything is negotiable. The contention of this session is that mentorship is *non-negotiable*. What principles from this session could you utilize to support this premise?

3. What evidence or principles would you use to tactfully persuade a senior leader who believes success is *self-made* of the importance of creating a practicable mentorship program both for personal and organizational growth?

4. What is your personal plan for using the principles in this session to support continued growth as a leader/mentor?

5. It has been stated that *purposeful relationships* inspire or move me to *accountability* that evolves and becomes my *professional responsibility*. You are aware that many of your peers have never had a mentor. How would you adapt the preceding concept to fit your workplace environment?

Quotes of Principled Leaders

"Education is the mother of leadership."
Wendell Lewis Wilkie

"I am personally convinced that one person can be a change catalyst, a transformer in any situation, any organization. Such an individual is yeast that can leaven an entire loaf. It requires vision, initiative, patience, respect, persistence, courage, and faith to be a transforming leader."
Stephen R. Covey

"Outstanding leaders go out of their way to boost the self-esteem of their personnel. If people believe in themselves, it's amazing what they can accomplish."
Sam Walton

"The most dangerous leadership myth is that leaders are born and that there is a genetic factor to leadership. This myth asserts that people simply either have certain charismatic qualities or not. That's nonsense; in fact, the opposite is true. Leaders are made rather than born." Warren G. Bennis
"No man will make a great leader who wants to do it all himself, or to get all the credit for doing it."
Andrew Carnegie

SESSION II

BUILDING BRIDGES OF CHANGE FOR ORGANIZATIONAL EFFECTIVENESS

Foundation

The oldest stone arch bridge in America was constructed in 1697 and still exists at Frankford Avenue over Pennypack Creek on U.S. Route 13 in Philadelphia, Pennsylvania. Mr. James Finley (1756–1828), is credited with inventing America's first suspension bridge out of iron chains in Uniontown Pennsylvania 1796. On November 7, 2008, the Pennsylvania Historical and Museum Commission (PHMC) dedicated an official state historical marker commemorating the bicentennial of the first U.S. suspension bridge patent granted to Finley in Uniontown. Neither this nor any of the nearly 40 bridges Finley constructed between 1808, when his patent was granted, and 1816, when wire cable suspension bridges made his iron chains obsolete, survives.[33]

Bridges are essential to travel and movement. Bridges cross rivers, canyons, or depressions in the land that otherwise are not possible to traverse. Bridges simply bring people and things together. According to history, although Mr. Finley was successful in building nearly 40 bridges, his success did not last because he was not able to change his building methods.

He had become accustomed to the way and pattern that had proven successful previously, and he was not able to change as change was occurring. To change is to, *"make the form, nature, or content of something different than what it once was. It also means to transform or convert; to exchange for something else."*[34] Change is about transformation or the process of "metanoia." Metanoia in its original Greek etymology means *"change of mind."* Metanoia further implies a journey (process) of changing one's minds, heart, self, or way of life. [35] Mr. Finley was quite effective in building bridges for a particular timeframe in Pennsylvanian history. Effectiveness, according to *The Oxford English Dictionary* is, *"the degree to which something is successful in producing a desired result."*

Although Mr. Finley's design and original pattern for bridges were successful and produced the desired

[33] http://www.portal.state.pa.us/portal/server.pt/community/historic_bridges/. Accessed February 17, 2015.

[34] www.dictionary.com. Accessed February 18, 2015.

[35] http://www.merriam-webster.com/dictionary/metanoia. Accessed February 17, 2015.

result, things were changing around him and he either did not notice or he did not pay attention to the changing environment. He lost his ability to be effective in building bridges. What is suggested in this session is that organizational effectiveness begins with the organization's capability and competency in *building bridges* with employees or team members. Every organization's endeavor is to be successful in what it provides to a particular community.

The behind-the-scenes technology operating in the organization and the products that are produced for customers always begin with people. An organization or company can have the most advanced technology available and possess the most sought-after product that is trending now, yet without the people behind it all, success and productivity will be minimal with the potential of becoming nonexistent or irrelevant.

From November 2008 to January 2009 *"Right Management,"* a company that focuses on workforce management, conducted a survey among its almost 29,000 employees from 10 major industry sectors in 15 countries in the Americas, Europe, and Asia-Pacific regions concerning organizational effectiveness. The survey asked participants to self-report on attitudes, performance, and conditions directly related to the effectiveness of their organization. [36] Most respondents (91%) were from private corporations employing 50 or more people, with revenues ranging

---

[36] Organizational Effectiveness. Discovering How To Make It Happen. Right Management Inc., Philadelphia, 2010, p. 3.

from under $1 million to over $1 billion. The study used a stratified sample of employees that matched the workforce population in each country on several factors, including industry, size of organization, gender, and age.

The survey further concluded, "*That in order to achieve increased and sustainable business results, organizations need to execute strategy and **engage employees**. To create organizational effectiveness, leaders need to focus on aligning and engaging their people, the people management systems, and the structure and capabilities (including organizational culture) to the strategy.*"

Strategy must always be forward thinking to remain relevant and productive. Strategy is a product of recognizing that change is coming. [37] As stated earlier, if change is inevitable, then how do we make change our ally for effectiveness within the organization? The answer is that we build bridges! Bridges are essential to *movement* and *progress* and are capable of bringing *ideals* and *people* together. When this occurs, progression is realized and productivity is increased because the ideal and the people have been brought together by the cooperative process of bridge building.

[37] IBID, p. 4.

Part I: Building the Bridge of Strategy

···

"In real life, strategy is actually very straightforward. You pick a general direction and implement. Strategy is an approximate course of action that you frequently revisit and redefine, according to shifting market conditions. It is an iterative process and not as theoretical as some would have you believe. When it comes to strategy, ponder less and do more."

Jack Welch

Businessdictionary.com defines strategy as, *"a method or plan chosen to bring about a desired future, such as achievement of a goal or solution to a problem"* and *"the art and science of planning and marshalling resources for their most efficient and effective use."* The term is derived from the Greek word *"strategos,"* which means *generalship* or the *leading* of an army. From the previous definition, there are three core elements of strategy. First, it is an *active process*, not just a design on a piece of paper. Second, it has *a focus or purpose* that lies in the future. It is a way to achieve a specific goal or set of goals. Finally, it involves *organizing people* and resources.

Sarah Weaver, president and owner of Strategic Creations, states, *"A strategy is directly correlated with 'action.' It is forward thinking; it is decisive; and it is* communicated to those that support and follow you."[38] In other words, having an idea is **not** a strategy. Ideas are simply goals. Planning the details and assigning accountability is how strategies are carried out and goals achieved. Additionally, Weaver states that a strategy is:

- Vision with action
- Endless Implementation
- Adaptive in order to achieve your goals [39]

If the strategy is to be successful, then every facet of the strategy must be seen through the lens of leadership, which from this perspective is creating, establishing, and executing goals. These goals may be financial goals, personal goals, or physical goals. For any organization or company, the right direction or where one aims to go is crucial to arriving at the desired destination. As a strategic leader, it is imperative that the factor of time is incorporated in gathering the necessary information to make an *informed* decision and not an *emotional* decision.

There are some matters that one may be confronted with that includes a great deal of emotion. This may be conflict between team members or financial matters that affect the organization. The strategic leader must *step back* and *step away* in order to *step forward*. To step

---

[38] http://strategiccreations.com/strategy-is-general-action-is-key/. Accessed February 17, 2015.
[39] IBID. Accessed February 17, 2015.

back is to step away from the situation to allow the emotionally charged moment to dissipate. Whatever time is necessary to allow the emotions to be cleared from the atmosphere will then allow the strategic leader to *step forward* and make an informed decision.

George Bernard Shaw once stated, "*The single biggest problem in communication is the illusion that it has taken place.*" Most of us think English, or our native language, and not communication in our relationships with others. We believe that because we have exchanged information that we have communicated, which is not always true.

The basic model of communication of the message, sender, receiver, and feedback is many times insufficient for effective communication. What must be included in the communication process are the elements of *time* and *accurate* information. The collecting of the necessary background information implies the element of time.

The strategic leader is a responsible, practiced, disciplined communicator. Communicating the shared roles and responsibilities to the right people from this perspective creates a greater platform of effectiveness organizationally.

If we get it right the first time, whatever the task or assignment may be, we will not have to do it a second time and waste both time and money. *Responsibility* means *accountability* for the resources of the company or organization. The strategic leader understands that he or she is responsible and accountable to not only the organization but to those they lead. This is building a bridge for greater success.

Consulting with one's leadership team is a pillar of strategic leadership. Consulting and including one's leadership team in the strategy for the future of the company or organization draws upon the collective skills of the team. No one can do what all of us can do. We are better together. A genuine *"we-ism"* takes the focus off of me because we are a team. In sports, championship teams draft the best available players based on their potential to contribute positively to the success of the team.

Regular consultation with one's leadership team allows every leader to contribute towards a greater strategy for the future. When inviting other people to be a part of one's team, the strategic leader certainly recognizes the strengths of the person. What may not be so clear are the weaknesses of a potential team member. It is easier to discuss a team member's strengths, as opposed to weaknesses. Every member of the team is different and therefore the strategic bridge builder is personally and relationally invested in overcoming organizational weaknesses through the combined strength of the team.

The strategic bridge builder always places members of the team in their greatest areas of strength. Teams who know each other's strengths and weaknesses allow team members to be open and honest with each other and draw upon the collective strengths to overcome any areas of weakness.

There are certainly many other facets that could be applied as a means of building a bridge of strategy within one's organization. Nevertheless, the principles of *vision with action, endless implementation,* and *adapting* in order to achieve organizational goals are a solid footing on which to begin the process.

PART II: BUILDING THE BRIDGE OF DIVERSITY

"Diversity maybe the hardest thing for a society to live with, and perhaps the most dangerous thing for a society to be without."

William Coffin Jr.

The European Territorial Cooperation (ETC) was created due to armed conflicts, complex border controls, and barriers erected between people and the lack of cooperation in Europe after the Second World War. As a result, the desire for economic and political union in Europe grew stronger. In the 1950s, French Foreign Minister Robert Schuman set out to create an even closer union among the peoples of Europe by helping countries and regions to cooperate for the benefit of all.

The aim and goal of the ETC is *"cooperation across the continent through the exchange of ideas and working towards common goals, as opposed to reinventing the wheel."*[40] By this initiative, in essence, the European Territorial Cooperation (ETC) has *"built a bridge"* for different people and nations for collaboration or improvement of the region. The aim of the European Territorial

---

40 http://ec.europa.eu/regional_policy/sources/information/pdf/brochures/etc_book_lr.pdf, p. 3. Accessed February 23, 2015

Cooperation is the construction of a *"common European space, and to build a cornerstone for European integration."*[41]

Integration in its simplest definition is "an act of combining different elements into a part of the whole."[42] Although team members may be on the team, what creates a greater value is the knowledge that *"I am included and I matter."* This is the place where building a bridge of people and processes declares by deliberate acts that our diversity is our greatest strength and not our greatest weakness in the organization. The ETC upholds and declares that there are common principles and ideals that unite us all. This includes a *"cooperation for cohesion"* among differing cultures, languages, and history, or the celebration and not simply the toleration of diversity.

The aim of ETC is to help ensure that borders are not barriers and that it is bringing people closer together, helping to solve common problems, facilitating the sharing of ideas and assets, and encouraging strategic work towards common goals. [43] The principles of the ETC initiative have great relevance for building bridges of change for organizational effectiveness. The ETC was birthed out of the conflict, chaos, and destruction of the Second World War over 70 years ago. Of great significance for consideration is the ETC's *"cooperating for cohesion, the solving of common problems, and the sharing of ideas, that lead us to common*

---

41 IBID, p. 8 Accessed February 23, 2015.

[42] www.dictionary.com. Accessed February 23, 2015.

[43] IBID, p. 9.

goals." Cohesion in its simplest definition is the act of uniting or sticking together.

Cooperation is the act of working together for a common purpose or benefit. William Arthur Wood once stated, *"Leadership is based on inspiration and not domination. On cooperation and not intimidation."*[44] What Wood suggests for bridge builders is that inspiration and cooperation are the path of least resistance, which further suggests that cooperating for cohesion is a matter of leadership. The act of uniting team members to work together for a common purpose is an act of one's leadership influence.

Whatever boundaries or barriers a person may have experienced prior to becoming a member of your team, based on their diverse backgrounds and cultures, the competent leader must take on the task of making a team out of individuals. The ETC was birthed out of chaos, conflict, and destruction. No matter what organization or company we belong to, it remains a matter for leadership to bring people together for the common goal of the company and the team.

A leader who is practiced in building bridges of diversity becomes a student of the backgrounds (culture, religion, etc.) of every employee or team member. Leaders ask questions such as, *"What types of barriers have the potential to separate or divide my team?" If cultural or diversity issues arise, am I prepared to defuse the*

---

[44] http://www.quotes.net/quote/39845. Accessed December 20, 2015.

issue and reunify my team? The resolving of problems is certainly a vital part of cooperating for cohesion.

When leaders value the input of employees or team members, they are more likely to deal with the problem before it becomes a bigger problem. *The Concise Oxford Dictionary* (1995) defines a problem as *"A doubtful or difficult matter requiring a solution* and *something hard to understand or accomplish or deal with."* A very basic model of problem-solving is:

- Identifying the problem
- Structuring the problem
- Looking for possible solutions to the problem
- Making a decision concerning the problem

Problems do not get better as they age. The longer a problem persists, the more discord it can create among the team. Building a shared responsibility for success within the ethos of the organization includes solving the problems. When problems arise, the principle of sharing of ideas is a part of structuring the problem. This aspect of problem-solving requires getting more information and understanding about the nature of the problem. This is about fact-finding and analysis or answering the question, *"What specifically has made this a problem for us?"*

Our cooperation with one another in every aspect of the operation, (the good and bad) of our organization further establishes the unity that is a part of our diversity.

Similar to the aim and goal of the ETC, a report from the Commission on Integration and Cohesion, "Our Shared Future," was published on June 14, 2007, and the Local Government Association (Britain) stated that community cohesion (cooperation) is an agreement on core values and principles considered necessities for sustainable community harmony and togetherness.

An important phrase from the Commission's perspective is *"Respecting differences, but developing a shared sense of belonging and purpose."*[45] The aim is to encourage more personal and collective knowledge of peoples around us, particularly people from different cultures, people of different ethnicities and faiths, people from different countries, people who are or appear to be different from ourselves.[46] The commission stated that a cohesive community is one where:

- There is a common vision and a sense of belonging for all.
- The diversity of people's different backgrounds and circumstances is appreciated and positively valued.
- Those from different backgrounds have similar life opportunities.

[45] http://www.leicestershiretogether.org/what_is_community_cohesion.pdf. Accessed February 24, 2015.
[46] IBID. Accessed February 24, 2015.

What is noted in the principles taken from the ETC and the Commission on Integration and Cohesion mode of operation are concerted efforts to bring people together or to build bridges. Inclusion is a place of belonging for everyone in the organization. As noted earlier, integration in its simplest definition is *"an act of combining different elements into a part of the whole."* Every part of a whole team is diverse and distinct. Organizational effectiveness begins with the organization's capability and competency in building bridges with employees and team members.

As leaders make the effort to build bridges of diversity, where a sense of belonging, value, and opportunity is available for every member of the team, issues that once had the potential to divide are now a part of the foundation of an organizational bridge that unites.

Part III: Building the Bridge of Structure and Capability

....

"The wisdom of bridges comes from the fact that they know both sides of the divide."
Mehmet Murat ildan (Turkish Playwright)

Organizational structure is a system used to define a hierarchy within an organization. It identifies each job, its function, and how each component fits into the overall framework of the organization. This structure is developed to establish how an organization operates and assists an organization in obtaining its goals to allow for future growth.

The Community Tool Box, a service of the Work Group for Community Health and Development at the University of Kansas, adds, *"Structure is the framework around which a group is organized, or the underpinnings which keep the coalition functioning. Structure is the operating manual that tells members how the organization is put together and how it works. More specifically, structure describes how members are accepted, how leadership is chosen, and how decisions are made."*[47]

In a *centralized* structure, the senior leadership also has the most responsibility for the success in operation of the organization simply because this is where all of the decisions are made. Typically, these are the

---

[47] http://ctb.ku.edu/en/table-of-contents/structure/organizational-structure/overview/main. Accessed February 23, 2015.

persons who have the most experience and tenure and therefore have earned their positions as senior leaders among many by *"coming through the ranks."* However, depending on the size of the organization, pertinent or critical information may not always reach the senior leaders because of this particular structure. Senior leaders have to depend upon other leaders at different levels in the organization to ensure that they have the information needed to make the best decisions that affect the organization's operation and success. [48]

In a *decentralized* structure of decision-making power distributed in the departments and divisions, with different degrees of independence, leaders are trusted to make the right decision for the organization and its people.[49]

In both a centralized and decentralized structures, the bottom line is *"people work before paperwork."* The administration of the organization's mission and standards are what make the company. Yet without the people, the standards and mission accomplishment will be hindered and impaired. People are hired to do the work, but in order for the *"paperwork"* (administration and operation), we must first be successful in *"people work."* This is where the leadership consistently and persistently works at relationships with team members and employees. Evaluation of a

---

[48] http://smallbusiness.chron.com/meaning-organizational-structure-3803.html. Accessed December 20, 2015.
[49] IBID, December 20, 2015.

team member's contribution to the organization is not something that should be done simply once a quarter or once a year. The *"people work"* is the work of the relationship in knowing with reasonable certainty, what a team member is capable of doing, or not capable of doing. *The Online Etymology Dictionary,* in its Late Latin root (1555–1565) says that the word "capable" originates from *"capabilis"* meaning *"able to grasp or hold."*[50]

If a team member or employee is not able to grasp or hold on to accomplishing a particular assignment, it does not necessarily mean that he or she is incompetent: A heart surgeon is quite competent in his or her field of expertise. Due to years of training and years of experience they are qualified and capable to perform of performing the surgery.

Of equal importance in this process of open-heart surgery is the anesthesiologist. During the surgery the anesthesiologist's job is to keep the patient safe and comfortable during surgery and recovery. The anesthesiologist keeps the patient asleep or unconscious during surgery by administering the appropriate drugs.

Although the anesthesiologist is a medical doctor and capable in the field of anesthetics, he or she is not capable or competent in performing heart surgery. The mission that brings this team of doctors and

---

[50] www.etymonline.com. Accessed February 23, 2015.

nurses together is to accomplish a successful open-heart surgery for the patient.

Each member of that particular team needs each other's skill set in order to accomplish the assignment of the surgery. Structure and standards are in place to ensure the safety of the patient and the utilization of the competencies of each member of the team. This simply means the right people in the right place doing the right things with the right competencies. Senior leadership, mid-level leadership, and junior leadership must find the balance between the proper structure and capabilities of individual team members.

Discovering and grooming emerging and potential leaders to ensure that the standards of the organization are secure is a never-ending task for leaders at every level.

Building a bridge of structure and capabilities that fits one's organization (never a one-size-fits-all situation), provides a platform for knowing both sides of the bridge: both the necessity of the right structure and the capabilities of the team.

The right *structure*, the right *people*, the right *competencies* in the right *place* are sure to foster organizational effectiveness.

PART IV: BUILDING THE BRIDGE OF TEAM COMMITMENT

....

"You've only got three choices in life: give up, give in, or give it all you've got."
            Title Boxing Club, Cottonwood Heights, Utah

Founded in 2008 by retired professional boxer Danny Campbell, Title Boxing Club is a health club with over 141 locations around the United States. The company is currently ranked No. 230 on 2015's *Entrepreneur* magazine 35th Annual Franchise 500 list, No. 9 on the magazine's prestigious 2014 "Top New Franchise" list, and No. 36 on the 2014 "Fastest Growing Franchise" list.[51] The workouts at any of the Title Boxing Clubs around the country are approximately one-hour sessions. The exercises involved in the workout sessions mirror those of a kickboxer or boxer.

High-energy cardio and strength training that burn over a thousand calories per session have become the trademark of Title Boxing Club. The sessions are intense and demanding, but no matter what a person's fitness goals maybe, the trainers encourage the participants that *"It can be done."*

I had to try it for myself, and once I did, the trainers certainly made a believer out of me. The sessions are indeed intense and demanding, but it can be done!

[51] http://titleboxingclub.com/wp-content/uploads/2013/05/Franchise_500_2014-FINAL_Approved. Accessed February 25, 2015.

What I learned from the first session in which I participated is that like any other endeavor in life, it is a person's level of commitment that produces the desired results.

During the one-hour sessions, the trainers' responsibility is to motivate and model the exercises for us as participants. My role as a participant was to commit to and follow the lead of the trainer in doing the exercises. The trainer was not responsible for my results as they depended upon my own level of commitment and desire to improve my physical condition. Commitment defined is the *"act of engaging, or pledging oneself."* In employee or team member commitment, Martin Maher discusses the necessity of *"personal investment."*

Maher says that the term implies a certain personal identification that involves loyalty or staying with the organization through thick and thin. Second, the term implies a willingness to put forth one's best efforts in making the organization work.[52] Maehr goes on to say that personal investment includes the job situation, the task to be done, or the role to be played. However, the preceding is not the sole determining feature of the context for personal investment. The nature, structure, policies, goals, and values of the organization make a difference. With this, Maher believes *"leaders can affect the context in which their staff works."*[53] His position

---

[52] https://www.ideals.illinois.edu/bitstream/handle/2142/7639/librarytrendsv38i1, p. 5. Accessed February 27, 2015.
[53] IBID, p. 6.

is that every team member has talent and energy to commit.

To engage this energy of commitment, an important factor is that team members *know* that as leaders we are as *equally* committed to them as we are asking them to be to us and the organization. This becomes a matter of loyalty from the leadership to the team membership. Most, if not all, organizations are looking for employees to be loyal without completely understanding that employees are also looking for organizations to be loyal to them as well! It is unreasonable and unrealistic to expect to receive loyalty that is not first given.

Considering this context of team commitment another vital component is producing or creating an atmosphere of job satisfaction so that team members will not look for another place to take their talents because they are treated extremely well in their current place of employment.

Every year, each of our professional sports teams have trading deadlines. Owners and coaches make an effort to improve their teams by moving a player to another team and getting a different player for the one that they traded. In some of those conversations, undoubtedly the mindset privately by the player or coaching staff is that this trade is not *personal, it's just business.* Maybe a player did not fit as well into a particular team's system or philosophy as the coaches or owners expected and the aim is to win. To do so, we need the right players, so we need to broker a trade.

In 100 years of Major League Baseball, according to Elias Sports Bureau, only 62 players with at least 15 years in the Major Leagues played their entire career with one organization.[54]

Five-time NBA championship winner Kobe Bryant of the Los Angeles Lakers states, *"It's very hard to find in this generation of sports an athlete that stays with one team the whole time. That's always been my dream as a kid, I've always felt like that's how it should be. Everybody likes what they like, but for me it's really important to stay with one team."*[55]

Creating the mindset organizationally that every member of the team is valuable to the success of the organization goes a long way in maintaining a "one team mentality." Being treated fairly and respected for one's contributions are organizational attributes that further concretize bridges of commitment for leaders and team members. The business perspective is certainly well understood. If a business is not making money, it won't be a business or organization for long. The average NBA team is now worth $1.1 billion, 74% more than last year. It is the biggest one-year gain since Forbes began valuing teams in the four major U.S. sports leagues in 1998.[56] According to Forbes, the average player's salary in the NBA is $5.15 million. In

---

[54] http://m.mlb.com/news/article/16083622/. Accessed February 28, 2015.
[55] http://www.lakersnation.com/lakers-news-kobe-says-its-important-to-him-to-stay-with-one-team/2013/08/12/. Accessed February 28, 2015.
[56] http://www.forbes.com/sites/kurtbadenhausen/2015/01/21/average-nba-team-worth-record-1-1-billion-2/. Accessed February 28, 2015.

MLB, it is $3.2 million, the NHL $2.4 million, and the NFL $1.9 million.[57]

The *business* aspect both for the organization and team member will always be a part of the discussion. Providing for one's family both now and in the future is always a consideration. However, if we can simply agree to pay a person what he or she is worth and get money off of the table, perhaps we can get closer to the *personal* dimension of the relationship, which does not have to be in opposition to the other.

In order to maintain the best team members available, there is a cost that organizations must be willing to pay. This is the business dimension. The personal cost investment is just as critical. If a team member believes and understands that it is more than just business, but personal in the sense that the organization or company to which he belongs genuinely cares about him and his family, authentic commitment becomes much more achievable.

What this means for the leadership is to find out the personal goals (career/financial) of team members and ensure that their goals tie into the organization's goals in order that *both* may be achieved. When team members do well personally, the company or business does well corporately.

Creating environments that are mutually beneficial become like steel in building bridges of team

---

[57] http://www.forbes.com/sites/monteburke/2012/12/07/average-player-salaries-in-the-four-major-american-sports-leagues/. Accessed February 28, 2015.

commitment. This will affect the context positively as team members work will always have the necessary motivation and commitment needed for effectiveness. This is how leaders bridge the gap between the business and the personal and team members live the experience of the actualization of a bridge built of commitment to the organization and commitment to the members of the team.

Summation: Building Bridges of Change for Organizational Effectiveness

In the foundation of this session, we discussed Mr. James Finley who was successful in building nearly 40 bridges in Pennsylvania. However, his success did not last because he was not able to change his methods. He had become accustomed to the way and pattern that had proven successful previously and was not able to change, even as change was occurring around him. Change is inevitable and change is consistent. Building bridges of change for organizational effectiveness is not a one-time endeavor. As the organization grows, change is occurring within the growth. The change may be very subtle or the change may be quite overt. To change is to *"make the form, nature, or content of something different than what it once was. It also means to transform or convert; to exchange for something else."*[58] Change is about transformation or the process of "metanoia." Metanoia in its original Greek etymology means *"change of mind."* Metanoia further implies a journey (process) of changing one's minds, heart, self, or way of life. The metaphor of bridge building is a means for preparing and creating a strategy of organizational effectiveness within the constancy of change.

---

[58] www.dictionary.com. Accessed February 18, 2015.

Businessdictionary.com defines strategy as *"a method or plan chosen to bring about a desired future, such as achievement of a goal or solution to a problem"* and *"The art and science of planning and marshalling resources for their most efficient and effective use."* The term is derived from the Greek word *"strategos,"* which means *generalship* or the *leading* of an army.

From the previous definition, there are three core elements of strategy. First, it is an *active process*, not just a design on a piece of paper. Second, it has a *focus* or *purpose* in the future. Strategy is a way to achieve a specific goal or set of goals. Third, it involves organizing or bringing people and resources together. The strategic leader is a responsible, practiced, disciplined communicator. Asking the right questions and communicating the shared roles and responsibilities to the right people from this perspective, creates a greater platform of effectiveness organizationally.

The basic model of communication of the message, sender, receiver, and feedback many times is insufficient for effective communication. What must be included in the communication process are also the elements of time and accurate information. Anything less may cause confusion and uncertainty.

William Coffin Jr. said, *"Diversity maybe the hardest thing for a society to live with, and perhaps the most dangerous thing for a society to be without."*

Diversity initiatives became so important that the European Territorial Cooperation (ETC) constructed a *"common European space and built a cornerstone for integration."*[59] Integration in its simplest definition is *"an act of combining different elements into a part of the whole."*[60] The dictionary says that a cornerstone is that which is the starting place; essential and indispensable to the foundation of the thing. The ETC upholds and declares that there are common principles and ideals that unite us all. This includes a *"cooperation for cohesion"* among differing cultures, languages, and history or the celebration and not simply toleration of diversity. A leader who has practiced building bridges of diversity becomes a student of the backgrounds (culture, religion, etc.) of every employee or team member. A leader asked questions such as, *"What types of barriers have the potential to separate or divide my team?"* Organizational effectiveness calls for the ability that if cultural or diversity issues arise, am I prepared to defuse the issue and reunify my team? What structures are in place to address these matters?

The University of Kansas says, *"Structure is the framework around which a group is organized, or the underpinnings which keep the coalition (organization) functioning."* In both a centralized and decentralized structure, the bottom line is that it must always be *"people work before paperwork."*

The administration of the organization's mission and standards are what make the company. Yet without the people, the standards and mission accomplishment will be hindered and impaired.

59 IBID, p. 8 Accessed February 23, 2015.
[60] www.dictionary.com. Accessed February 23, 2015.

People are hired to do the work, but in order for the *"paperwork"* (administration and operation) to work, we must first be successful in *"people work."* This is where the leadership consistently and persistently works at relationships with team members and employees that further solidify organizational effectiveness.

Concerning building bridges of team commitment, the motto of Title Boxing is *"It can be done."* The trainers consistently encourage participants that no matter what a person's fitness goals may be, it can be done. What I learned from the first session in which I participated is that like any other endeavor in life, it is a person's level of commitment that produces the desired results. Building bridges of team commitment can be done. It may not necessarily be an easy task, but professional boxers train to fight and to win a championship. A boxer after winning the championship has certainly earned a time of celebration because of the present success. However, if a champion wants to remain the champion, the celebration does not last too long. The training for maintaining the championship must continue. *"You've only got three choices in life: give up, give in, or give it all you've got."* (Title Boxing Club, Cottonwood Heights, Utah). In building bridges of team commitment, we want to give it all that we have.

The point of the matter is that we must, as leaders, continue to build bridges to ensure that the attitude of a champion is instilled in our team members and give it all that we've got. Achievement of this standard is animated by training for cohesiveness and guarding against any detrimental practices or attitudes that could corrode bridges or the standards that have brought us together. In so doing, organizational effectiveness is perpetually established, highly esteemed, and prepares us for the quest for the next championship.

Questions for Reflection

. . . .

1. How would you prove to others in your organization that a *metanoia* (change of mind) is necessary concerning some standard practices required to increase operational effectiveness?

2. The European Territorial Cooperation (ETC) was formed out of confusion and chaos. The intent of the coalition was to build a cornerstone of inclusion and cooperation for cohesion. If you believe that authentic inclusion cooperation and cohesion *does not* exist in your organization, as a competent leader, what steps do you take to begin the process of changing and ultimately eliminating these destructive patterns?

3. Strategy must always be forward-thinking to remain relevant and productive, as a product of recognizing that change is coming. What strategies do you believe are necessary for greater effectiveness in your *changing* organization for the future?

4. As a leader, you have several members of your team who have great potential but appear to be more committed to *self* than to the *team*. Which principles from this session could you use to accentuate the value of a *"one team mentality?"*

5. You know both the leaders and team members in your organization that by their attitude and

conduct are doing *"just enough"* to cooperate organizationally. What bridge-building steps will you incorporate to produce "more than enough" results in both attitude and conduct within the organization?

QUOTES OF PRINCIPLED LEADERS

"You can't change what is going on around you until you start changing what's going on within you."

Unknown

"The best leaders treat people the best."

Kent Julian

"The secret of change is to focus all of your energy not on the old, but on building the new."

Socrates

"Relationship means, relate to me on my ship."

G. L. Cruell

"If you are persistent, you will get it. If you are consistent, you will keep it."

Unknown

SESSION III

CREDIBILITY—THE KEY TO ORGANIZATIONAL CONFIDENCE

Foundation

Credibility is simply the quality of being believable or worthy of trust. The root of the word *"credibility"* is *"credo,"* which means *"I believe"* in its original Latin root.[61] Put simply, credibility is the feeling of trust and respect that a leader inspires in others that is believable. It is this type of credibility and believability that is the key to team members' confidence in their organization.

The *Oxford English Dictionary* defines confidence as the *"state of feeling certain about the truth of something; a full trust in something or someone."* People like to work with leaders who are truly confident. There is a natural tendency to trust people more when

---

[61] http://www.etymonline.com. Accessed March 21, 2015.

they appear confident. For most of us, dealing with a confident person assures us that the person is also competent. Generally, when a leader exhibits confidence, it makes it easier to trust that leader, and people want to work with leaders they trust, believe, and have confidence in the organization or company. Jack Welch, former CEO of General Electric stated, *"Self-confidence gives you courage and extends your reach. It lets you take greater risks and achieve far more than you ever thought possible."*[62]

Confidence and credibility create an organizational atmosphere where there is nothing that cannot be accomplished or achieved. In this type of environment, it is believability in the organization's credibility that will cause me to authentically follow thee as a leader.

[62] http://www.advisausa.com/wp-content/uploads/2011/10/CEOMay07.pdf. Accessed April 1, 2015.

PART I: BELIEVABILITY IS WHAT CAUSES ME TO FOLLOW THEE

In an Indiana cemetery, there lies a tombstone that reads: *"Pause, stranger, when you pass me by. As you are now, so once was I. As I am now, so you will be, prepare yourself to follow me.* An unknown passerby read those words and underneath scratched this reply: *"To follow you I'm not content, until I know which way you went."*[63] The anecdote provides a very important aspect of followership. Although stated in a somewhat humorous manner, there's a great deal of truth to be applied as well.

The person who was passing by was not swayed by the obvious admonishment. His reply suggested a belief in one of two destinations after life on earth. Whatever a person believes in has the power and potential for contentment. Contentment simply defined is satisfaction with what one has and not desiring more or anything else. To reach this place of contentment further suggests a belief in the path by which one arrived at this state. A translation of the moral of the anecdote is, *"If I'm going to follow you, I have to believe in the way you are going."*

In healthy organizations where employees or team members are valued, it is no longer about having a job

---

[63] http://billygraham.org/story/one-minute-after-you-die/. Accessed March 24, 2015.

to provide for one's family or well-being. There must be a belief in the way a company or organization is going. Job satisfaction creates a desire to be a contributing member or factor to the company's success and that further suggests a team member's belief in the product or service that the company provides. To retain the best team members or employees suggests that one must believe into what they are investing their time and talents. For some, money is no longer the most important factor. Many professional athletes in order to assist building the best possible team capable of winning a championship will take less money to attract or sign a player who will help them to win.

Most of us will not have the opportunity to be offered a multimillion-dollar contract for contributions to a team or company; however, the principle is still relevant. Believing in the organization is what will *"cause me to follow thee."* However, in following it is important that we are aware of and do not neglect our own personal values, beliefs and attitudes before we can adopt the values and beliefs of our industry or organization. What we believe in is valuable to us because it reflects who we are and how we conduct our lives.

What we believe are important qualities, or what qualities we admire in ourselves and others, generally reflect our life experiences and the values that we established in our early years through the influence of family, teachers, friends, religion, culture, or our education.

Closely related to our beliefs are our attitudes. The word *attitude* can refer to a lasting group of feelings, beliefs, and behavioral tendencies directed towards specific people, groups, ideas, or objects. An attitude is a belief about something. It usually describes what we think is the proper way of doing something. The attitudes that we feel very strongly about are usually caused by our values. Others' attitudes are sometimes not as important and are more like opinions and everyone has a right to their opinion. However, sometimes our own attitudes can make us blind to other people's values, opinions, and needs, which can be counter-productive to the needs of the organization.

Attitudes will always have a positive and negative element, and when you hold to a particular attitude, you will have a tendency to behave in a certain way towards that person or object. We all recognize that every member of the organization comes with an inculcated belief and value system. The beliefs and attitudes that a person possesses personally are one thing. The beliefs and attitudes that a person possesses concerning the organization or the company are another thing.

How then does the leader bring these two very divergent paths together? How does the leader accomplish the level of credibility or believability that will increase organizational productivity? Consider the *"power of professionalism."* Bill Wiersma and seven contributors from various leadership backgrounds in

2010 published the book, *"The Power of Professionalism."* In the book, the authors discuss *"seven mindsets that drive performance and build trust."*[64] According to Wiersma, a certain mindset reflects who *"a person is, not what a person does."*

In addition, a mindset is *"one part personal values, one-part emotional maturity, and one-part life's experience."*[65]

The seven mindsets are:

1. *Professionals Have a Bias for Results.*
2. *Professionals Realize (and Act Like) They're Part of Something Bigger than Themselves.*
3. *Professionals Know Things Get Better When They Get Better.*
4. *Professionals Have Personal Standards that Often Transcend Organizational Ones.*
5. *Professionals Know Personal Integrity Is All They Have.*
6. *Professionals Aspire to Be Masters of Their Emotions, Not Enslaved by Them.*
7. *Professionals Aspire to Reveal Value in Others.*[66]

A professional is one who is qualified and certified, normally after a particular course of study or years of preparation in a particular occupation as proficient

[64] Wiersma, Bill. The Power of Professionalism. The Seven Mind-Sets That Drive Performance and Build Trust (Los Altos: Ravel Media), 2010, 103.
[65] IBID, 280.
[66] http://www.wiersmaandassociates.com/blog/the-seven-mind-sets/. Accessed November 12, 2015

or knowledgeable. Becoming qualified (professional) in these seven mindsets has the potential and ability to further concretize organizational believability and credibility.

Adopting these seven mindsets assists in transcending temperament, social hierarchy, and intellectual prowess because they are *principle* centered, or true in any context, situation or environment.

A closer look at these seven mindsets suggests that they are just as applicable to seasoned veteran leaders as they are to those just entering the workforce. As universal principles, they are just as pertinent to a Wall Street firm, the medical community, a professional sports team, college or university, or religious organization. Leaders seek productivity, accountability, cohesiveness, and commitment to initiatives.

Creating an environment of professional credibility and confidence will also require cultivation or devotion to the practice of a *"culture of professionalism."*

Raising professional standards dramatically impacts all aspects and operations of the organization and therefore the character of the organization is revealed and respected, which further enhances believability. A particular culture reflects the values, customs, and traditions of its people. If an organization's culture reflects professionalism, consequently, it will produce the desired results of professionalism.[67] Therefore, professionalism and its accompanying mindset must be of *value* and *valuable* and practiced.

Although it would certainly be nice to purchase my wife of over 30 years a wedding ring with a price tag and value of $5 million, but the acquisition of that ring is probably not going to happen! If the ring went on sale for $1 million, the procurement of the ring is probably still not going to occur. What about $750,000? Even at this current sale price, the ring will most likely remain in the realm of probably never going to happen! The ring, although of value, is not within the realm of *my* cultural norm or experience. Realistically, at my current salary, it is not attainable and therefore is of no value (although valuable) to me personally. Everything that is of *value* is not necessarily *valuable* to all. Professional conduct and behavior must be both of *value* and *valuable* to a leader, and no price tag can be placed on the value of credibility gained with those that he or she leads when these traits are actualized.

Possessing the mindset of professionalism as suggested, reflecting and practicing ways that I can *get better* and *do better* will assist the process of solidifying credibility and believability organizationally.

[67] IBID, 280.

PART II: RELATIONSHIP—RELATE TO ME ON MY SHIP

··

Establishing or building the credibility of interpersonal relationships means that leaders must connect with team members or employees where they are. If each member of the team approaches their work relationships as if on a ship, one could be sailing to the Bahamas, while another is sailing to Europe! We are not going in the same direction, which will eventually produce problems organizationally. The first thing that must be achieved is to get everyone on the same *"relation-ship."*

As a leader, you are at the center of every relationship that matters and they *all* matter. Imagine the wheel of a bicycle in which you the hub or center and each spoke represents a relationship with another person. Does that sound egotistical? It doesn't need to be. It takes a lot of spokes to hold the wheel together and the wheel is what helps move organizational goals along. The competent leader has to take the time to set up and sustain relationships. If you wait for others to establish relationships with you first, you may spend a lot of time waiting! Some relationships require more time than others.

You may want to meet for lunch once or twice a month with your team members specifically for team building. Relationships are best built one at a time.

There are no short cuts. A monthly newsletter may help you as a leader to keep in touch with employees or team members, but it is no substitute for getting to know the people who you lead personally. Depending on a person's particular personality, many may feel that spending time on relationship building across the organization is not necessary. All that matters is that the *"job gets done."* This kind of isolationist thinking, although not seen outwardly, is to some extent like termites under the floorboards.

The *"out of sight"* destruction that these tiny insects create may take years to notice, but when the damage is finally noticed, it most likely will become an extreme financial burden to correct. However, establishing solid working relationships early within the organizational structure becomes like preventative maintenance to solving a problem or getting the job done. Building and sustaining solid, strong relationships is central to mission or project accomplishment. When you plan a project, you need to include the time it takes to build relationships into your plan. *People need time to build trust.* Whenever people work together, they need to have trusting relationships. When trust is missing, people usually have a difficult time functioning cooperatively.

Disagreements seem to erupt over no important reason. Investing time, resources, and one's reputation can be risky. At the very least, people want some return for their investment. They have to feel like you know them as a person, understand their interests, and as their leader, they want to know that *you will not let them down.*

How Do You Build Relationships?

A clear path to building relationships is by being a **R.A.T.** Forgive me for that mental picture that just appeared in your head! No, I'm not talking about a large rodent that resembles a mouse and neither am I referring to a person regarded as despicable, deceitful, or disloyal. The attributes of a **R.A.T.** are as follows:

- **R-**espected/Reliable
- **A-**ccountable/Ardent
- **T-**enacious/Tailored

Respected and Reliable

To be *respected* carries the meaning of a deep-rooted admiration as a result of a person's abilities, qualities, or achievements. To be *reliable* is to be trusted, accurate, and honest. With this, the competent leader is willing to *"tell others about themselves."* This is the leader attribute of vulnerability—an open, honest exchange about self with others. Being vulnerable also includes a certain level of maturity in understanding what to share and what not to share. It is not a time for confession.

It is an honest, forthright exchange of self-designed to help create trust for building real relationships. Superman and his cousin Supergirl are fictional comic book creations, and even with all of their "super powers," they also had their kryptonite or weaknesses. People won't trust you unless there is a belief that as a leader you are real and that you are willing to trust them just as they are. It is never about perfection.

It is about the process of being *perfected* or growing and in a respected, reliable relationship, we are growing together. Authentic respect and a sense of reliability will follow these types of exchanges.

Accountable and Ardent

Oftentimes, underneath the tough, independent exterior of a person is often a lonely soul hoping someone will *"relate to them on their ship"* or life experiences. Some have had to develop a tough exterior as a means of protection and self-preservation. An atmosphere of mutual accountability from the leader to the led can provide a venue that goes the extra mile in relationship building.

People are often suspicious. It takes a while to win or gain trust. You can almost always form a relationship if you stick with it. Assume other people want to form relationships, as well. People have a need to communicate even if they do not necessarily know it. When people don't have a chance to talk about important issues, misunderstandings can occur and tensions often build up.

Communication is a discipline that must be practiced regularly. Check in with people when you need to. This promotes accountability. This may take only a few minutes a week, but those few minutes can make the difference in helping your team members to remember the importance of the work you are doing together and as I am asking you to be accountable, so am I accountable to you.

Accountability means that you have the ability to count or to make a difference. This is leading from the front. It is not a *"do as I say"* mindset. No, from this position in front, what needs to be done, I do it with you and we are accountable to one another.

An ardent, passionate, leader expresses genuine appreciation for all. Everyone needs to be appreciated in order to keep healthy relationships alive.

This assists in bringing into existence an *"I want to be accountable"* way of thinking among team members. If you notice that someone did a stellar job for the organization, then say so publically! If an idea that improved client retention or reception of more customers was suggested by one of your team members, then let them know! To be ardent carries the idea of intense, enthusiastic devotion to a cause or someone. The competent leader never forgets that we are all human beings and a leader and organization that appreciates what individual team members bring to the table every day helps us all to stay alive and to thrive.

Tenacious and Tailored

Many suffer from a fear of rejection, and there's only one thing to do about that: *get over it!* As a competent leader, if you want to form relationships, plan on being *"rejected"* some of the time. As a leader, the aim is not *friendship* necessarily with superiors, team members, or employees; the aim is *relationships*. Yet when credible relationships are forged, out of the *relationship* will come *friendships* that will richly reward you as a leader and the organization.

A *tenacious*, unyielding focus on relationship building does not distract the competent leader from the minimal rejections of a few toward this operational standard. To be *tailored* is that which fits the person or the situation. If as a leader all you are acquainted with is *"small, medium or large size"* responses, depending on the severity of the matter at hand, there are a lot of people and situations that are somewhere "in between." A team member who is 5"1 and 135 pounds is not going to fit into the same suit that someone 6"4 and 235 pounds wears.

One size fits all leadership just does not work. To be tailored requires *measurements* and *proximity*. What fits the person or a particular situation will be determined by the proximity or *shared closeness* in the relationship. There are just some things that employees or team members are not going to share with their leaders because of a lack of proximity or closeness.

Measured dialogue in the process of building the relationship will progressively assist to *close the proximity gap*. The competent leader can never assume that because someone works for or is employed by the organization that *"anything goes."* Even at a time of reprimand or correction, the competent leader never loses sight of the responsibility of measured dialogue. In other words, this is a restatement of the adage that we know as the "Golden Rule: *"Do unto others as you would have them do unto you."* In so doing the door or ability to tenaciously challenge each other to do better is actualized.

Organizational inspiration and motivation are assignments for all of us. If we believe in each other and the organization, then we help each other to stretch ourselves beyond what we think we can do.

This helps to build stronger relationships by challenging our work partners to take on bigger challenges. The tenaciously and tailored competent leader backs up each team member and the organization equally when things get tough. Loyalty is essential to keeping relationships healthy. We may not agree with co-workers or friends in every circumstance, but we can stand by them when they are in a jam.

Relationships and Conflict

There is no such thing as *"organizational utopia "*or perfection. Conflict or differing perspectives will arise because we are all different and no one is perfect.

Misunderstandings or misinformation will most often lead to conflict that can further lead us to miscommunication, misjudgments, and mistakes. Many relationships, both personal and work, will be challenged, and that's not necessarily a bad thing. Conflict doesn't mean that the relationship has to come to an end. You may recall growing up that some of your biggest fights were with your brothers and sisters! Yet, at the end of the day, he was still your brother and she was still your sister. Someone that you loved and cared for intensely.

When conflict occurs, here are some ideas that may assist relationships in conflict:

- *Take time to listen to each other.* This is not always easy. Each person should take time some time to listen without interrupting, while the other person talks. This is listening for comprehension and not waiting for your opportunity to respond.
- *Put yourself in the other person's shoes.* Everyone in a conflict has distinctly different views of a situation. In the thick of a fight, people are usually convinced they are absolutely right. Train yourself to see why the other person sees things the way they do. Just your attempt to do so will help the other person see your effort in solidifying this relationship.
- *Look at what is true about what the other person is saying.* See if you can correct the

situation. If you need to apologize, go ahead and do it! Humility in leadership expressed in an apology can often help a relationship get back on the right track.

- *Separate emotions from reality.* Everyone has emotions that surface intermittently. People often say things they don't mean when they are in the middle of an emotional upheaval. How I respond at any given moment in this exchange must be viewed through the lens of "fiction or fact."

- My emotions (fiction or non-fiction) can cloud reality and obscure my objectivity or the facts of the matter.

- *Speak from your heart.* As you try to unravel the difficulty, keep focused on what you and the other person care about most: the goals of the project, each other, the community, and the organization.

- *Don't give up your principles.* Don't sacrifice what you believe in just to make a relationship work. If you give up on your principles, you won't be effective and the relationship won't work anyway.

- *You can act independently to improve any relationship.* Even if the other person or group of people is acting contrary to organizational goals, you can act in a way that is positive, respectful, constructive, and thoughtful.

Relationship building may be challenging, but it is not impossible. Understanding relationships is no simple task. People are so unique and complex that there is no easy formula. Central to almost every major religion around the world is the idea that we should treat our neighbors the way we would like to be treated.

By keeping the golden rule in mind, the competent leader will most likely succeed in building relationships that are dependable and reliable. Building and sustaining relationships are at the heart of healthy, growing, and organizing communities. The strength of organizational credibility and believability lies in the strength of the connections (relationships) that we have with each other.

With relationships like these, people have the power to make real change. Building these connections takes time and real, authentic efforts. Libby Chase, in an article written for *Young Money* says, "*Reality TV now makes up **17 percent of prime time TV programming. So the question that Chase addresses is, how real is reality TV?** The answer? Not very.*" Chase goes onto say, any time you follow someone around with a camera, it ceases to be "*reality*" as most real people don't live their lives in front of cameras. Second, any time you create an environment, such as putting a bunch of strangers into a house, it ceases to be reality.

Real-life friends are often exchanged for better-looking fake friends. Situations are created. In short, stories are formed. Reality story editors or segment producers also write jokes, script the back-and-forth banter for hosts and *"shape"* the participants' conversations. Chase goes on to say that *"these environments are completely created, they are artificial, meaning, they are not real."*[68]

People trust what they believe to be real and authentic. This is birthed from the truth of a morality that is unmoved by the status quo. Authentic leaders genuinely desire to serve others through their leadership. They are more interested in empowering the people they lead to make a difference than they are in power, money, or prestige for themselves.

To become authentic, each of us has to develop our own leadership style consistent with our personality and character. To create an organizational structure of credibility, believability, and authenticity, team members or employees at some point may ask the question, *"Is this for real?"* Another way to answer this question is to review the idea of what makes an authentic leader or a believable leader. It is one thing to have the values and aims of organizational unity and cohesiveness in the employee manual. It is another thing for people to *authentically* experience the values and aims of organizational unity and cohesiveness when they show up to work every day.

Authentic credible leaders have the task of engaging the hearts of those he or she serve and aligning their interests with the interests of the organization. To

---

[68] finance.youngmoney.com/careers/how-much-does-reality-tv-pay/. Accessed March 23, 2015.

engage in the hearts of others requires a sense of purpose and an understanding of where you're going. When you find that alignment, you and your team have the power to move mountains. Nothing will be able to stop the momentum of an organization of this nature.

A continued exploration and pursuit of authenticity, interwoven with credibility and believability, will consistently bring us back to the place of starting for a leader (influence) and to know that place for the first time. For without authenticity, it is possible that our credibility is insufficient and therefore lacks believability.

PART III: CONFIDENCE THAT CULTIVATES HOPE FOR THE FUTURE

The *Oxford English Dictionary* says that confidence is, "*the mental attitude of trusting in or relying on a person or thing. Confidence is a firm trust, reliance, or faith. The feeling of assurance, certitude; assured expectation.*"

Agriculturally, cultivation is that which ensures health and growth of that which has planted to produce a desired crop. This includes the soil, proper nutrients, and a sufficient water supply to ensure that the planted seed does not die or dry out from thirst. Using the preceding as a metaphor, cultivating hope for the future primarily means that credible leaders have the responsibility for the health and well-being of their team to produce the services or products of the organization. Credible leaders impart into members of their team continual "organizational nourishment" in order to survive and thrive in any and every environment.

Cultivating hope for the future is part of legacy and perpetuity. As a means of creating confidence and credibility in this aim, a tremendous ally is the utilization of a *"cause driven leadership model"* such as utilized by the YMCA. Cause-driven leadership is the practice of leading in a manner that advances our cause to strengthen communities through our work in youth development, healthy living, and social responsibility.

Every day, cause-driven leaders think, act, and communicate with the needs of their community front and center and in ways that drive our desired impact. It is the YMCA's belief that a strong community can only be achieved when we invest in our kids, our health and our neighbors.[69] The cause driven model of leadership consists of 4 components:

- Mission Advancement
- Collaboration
- Operational Effectiveness
- Personal Growth

Investing in youth, health, and our neighbors continues to strengthen the concept of community. Within the organization, the idea of community is a vital component of unit cohesiveness. As the call of the YMCA fits this ideal, so should it be within our organizations. The youth represent new hires to the organization. The health of the organization represents an understanding of our responsibility personally and to other members of the team of the value of the *"cause."*

The cause is what helps to maintain the focus of the purpose of the organization. In the YMCA model, the cause is ultimately the *"strength of the community."*

[69] http://ymcachgo.3cdn.net/75ca679fb34c9b370c_vbm6bvfgi.pdf. Accessed March 26, 2015.

The community is made up of our neighbors and our neighbors in this concept are those we work with.

The cause of cultivating hope for the future organizationally is to create confidence in the future. In 1985, actor Michael J. Fox starred in the very successful movie, *"Back to The Future."* In the movie, Michael's character Marty, via the flux capacitor and his DeLorean, was able to travel to the future and back. In his journey, Marty discovered different versions of the future and when he discovered life circumstances in the future not to his liking, his aim was to go back in time to produce the desired future. Through the eyes of Marty, the movie in a very entertaining manner, helps us to see what was desired by Marty for his future. Traveling back and forth through time, Marty was determined to get his *"future right."*

A very familiar term among many leadership circles is that of *"carpe diem."* Carpe diem is usually translated from its Latin origins as *"seize the day."* However, the more precise Latin scholars state that *"carpe"* translates literally as *"pluck"* with particular reference to the picking of fruit, so a more accurate rendition of carpe diem is *"enjoy the day, pluck the day when it is ripe."* [70]

Without the time machine that Marty had in *"Back to The Future,"* it will be very difficult for us to get *"the future right"* because we have not yet arrived in our future! However, the idea or concept of carpe diem

---

[70] http://www.phrases.org.uk/meanings/carpe-diem.html. Accessed March 26, 2015.

provides us with a platform for focusing on the reality of the here and the now. There are opportunities in the present, the here and now, that when *"plucked when they are ripe,"* will become a part of the process of cultivating and nourishing the people that we lead and the products and services that the organization provides in the future.

This is by no means suggests that we should not consider the future. Long-range planning and short-term planning are critical concepts for looking towards and being prepared for the future. It is not an either or proposition; it is acknowledging the reality of both perspectives. When there is a balance of both the present realties and future possibilities, there is an inherent and external hope created that arises among team members throughout the organization that breeds optimism.

John William Gardner served as the Secretary of Health, Education, and Welfare under President Lyndon B. Johnson. He also founded Common Cause. He was president of the Carnegie Foundation and established the White House Fellows Program. He served as Consulting Professor at the School of Education at Stanford. He served under six U.S. presidents. He chaired, taught, led, inspired, wrote, mentored, thought, and acted out his life in public service.

As a former cabinet member, John W. Gardner said, *"The first and last task of a leader is to keep hope alive—the hope that we can finally find our way through to a better world—despite the day's action, despite our own inertness, shallowness, and wavering resolve."*[71]

At every level of leadership and influence in which he served, Mr. Gardener's legacy *"spoke hope"* and optimism. As a candle that produces light in dark places, so does hope produce light in times of stress and difficulties. It is the light of hope that helps us find our way to *"a better world"* through it all.

Since 1935, The Gallup Poll has chronicled reactions to the events that have changed our world and, in turn, those reactions have shaped who and what we are today. For more than 70 years, Gallup has built its reputation on delivering relevant, timely, and visionary research on what humans around the world think and feel. No other organization captures the human need to share opinions and the breadth of the human spirit like The Gallup Poll. [72] Shane Lopez, a psychologist, serves as a senior scientist for Gallup and research director of the Clifton Strengths Institute. He is also a fellow of the American Psychological Association.

In his book, *Making Hope Happen: Create the Future You Want for Yourself and Others,* Shane Lopez says that hope can be learned and hopeful people share four core beliefs:

- The future will be better than the present.
- I have the power to make it so.

---

[71] https://studentaffairs.stanford.edu/haas/about/haasprofessorship/johngardner. Accessed March 26, 2015.
[72] http://www.gallup.com/poll/101905/gallup-poll.aspx. Accessed March 31, 2015.

- There are many paths to my goals.
- None of them is free of obstacles. [73]

The Future Will Be Better than the Present

Hope is defined as the feeling that what is wanted can be had or that events and circumstances will turn out for the best. Hope is further defined as a desire for something and the possibility of its fulfillment. When we choose to hope, it becomes a defining moment as to what matters to us most. These four core beliefs about hope are the place where one seeks out and identifies where we want to go, want to accomplish, and who we want to be.

It does not matter if it is tomorrow over a lifetime. Hope is built from the goals that matter most to us. The aspirations that we come back to again and again that fill our minds with pictures of the future.[74]

Hope is a choice and someone once said, *"The choices of yesterday is what has made us who we are today."* As we take responsibility for moving towards our goals, we develop our ability to motivate ourselves, and we build our capacity for persistence and long-term effort.

According to Lopez, each element of the hope cycle interacts with the others in ways that can reinforce, modify, or diminish the other. Each element is strong,

[73] Lopez, Shane. Making Hope Happen: Create the Future You Want For Yourself and Others. (New York: Atria Books) 2013, 18-19.
[74] IBID, 24.

and together they form a cycle that enhances hope. When even one element of the cycle is weak, hope diminishes until there is intervention to strengthen the element that is undeveloped or faltering.[75] Also in this cycle of hope, Lopez talks about a principle that he utilizes or practices with his seven-year-old son that he calls *"nexting."*

In nexting, he talks with his son about the *next* basketball game, the *next* movie we will watch, or the *next* family trip. It is a way of practicing hope with his son. By encouraging his son to talk about the future, he discovers what his son is excited about. In this way, Lopez states, he learns about his son's plans for what is next in his life, and this helps him to come up with ideas about how to make all of the *next* things happen." Lopez further adds that talking about the next important event in his son's life allows him as his father to gauge whether he is confident or fearful. Lopez's principle of *nexting* is a tool of evaluation. With our successes or failures how do we gauge what is *next?*

How do the plans that we have lined up for today complement and work with our thoughts of tomorrow? What is the *next* phase of leader and team development that I can initiate that will increase productivity and elevate hope for the future? Not only does this principle suggest *evaluation* but it also suggests *evolution.* As I honestly evaluate the present, the evaluation reveals

---

[75] IBID, 25.

the *next* opportunity for continued growth. We never stop growing, and we never stop learning. Hope can be either *ethereal* or *practical*. The competent credible leader chooses to make hope practical concerning a future that will be better than the present because I have the power to make it so.

I Have the Power to Make It So

Lopez adds the following statement to undergird or support this component of the hope cycle: "*Five years ago… five years from now.*" In its proper and full context, the question is: "*Five years ago, did you see yourself here?*" The second question in its full context is: "*Five years from now, what do you want your life to look like?*"[76] In a technique that Lopez utilizes to reinforce hope in clients, students and colleagues when celebrating a recent success or meaningful accomplishment, he asks the question, "*Five years ago, did you see yourself here?*" Lopez goes on to say that, in retrospect, many smile and talk about the hard times and obstacles they overcame to arrive at the present success or accomplishment.

Many reflect upon the combination of desire and determination and the hope that had arisen during that timeframe. In other words, what Lopez suggests is that the ability to succeed was in a large part due to one's *own hope for the future that was within their own hands.*

---

[76] IBID, 92.

History records that Winston Churchill took a steamship through German submarine-infested waters around Christmas in 1941, just after the Empire of Japan attacked Pearl Harbor, drawing the U.S. into World War II. Addressing the U.S. Congress Churchill states, *"Sure I am that this day, now we are the masters of our fate; that the task which has been set us is not above our strength; that its pangs and toils are not beyond our endurance. As long as we have faith in our cause and an unconquerable will-power, salvation will not be denied us."*[77] An indomitable declaration of hope reflecting the mindset that together we have the ability to make it so by our own hands.

There Are Many Paths to My Goals

The United States Army trains and equips selected soldiers to be *Pathfinders*. The Pathfinders' distinctive winged torch symbol that they wear on their uniforms comes from ancient Greece where runners opened up the Olympic Games and the symbol means to *"Light the Way."*

A pathfinder is inserted or dropped into place in order to set up and operate drop zones, pickup zones, and helicopter landing sites for airborne operations, air resupply operations, or other air operations in support of the ground unit commander. Pathfinders first appeared in World War II and continue to serve an

[77] http://ghostsofdc.org/2012/03/14/the-masters-of-our-fate-winston-churchill-addresses-congress-1942/. Accessed March 31, 2015.

important role in today's modern military, providing commanders with the option of flexibly employing air assets.[78]

Stanford psychologist Carol Dweck in her studies of motivation, intelligence, and how we cope with failure, discusses two possible ways to think about intelligence and personality and how they relate to the future or the accomplishment of goals. Dweck utilizes the term *"mindset"* for those beliefs that we have about ourselves. Dweck goes on to say that if you have a *"fixed mindset,"* you believe that your abilities are set in stone – you have them or you don't. Dweck's research also says that if you have a fixed mindset, you are less hopeful about the future because this is as good as it gets. There's nothing you can do to change it, so why try?

If you have a *"growth mindset, "*you know and believe that you can develop your talents and build your abilities. You have nothing to lose, and much to gain, by pursuing new ways to reach your goals. [79]

Additional research by Lopez with his colleagues that include psychologists and educators from around the world advocates that the science of hope shows that *how we think about the future is a key determinant of success in school, work, and life,* which supports Dweck's concept of a growth mindset. In other words, the growth and practice of hope relates to academic

---

[78] http://www.benning.army.mil/infantry/rtb/1-507th/pathfinder/content/pdf/pathfinder%20history.pdf. Accessed March 31, 2015.
[79] Lopez, 98.

success, better business outcomes, and well-being. Lopez's research indicates that hope leads to a 12% gain in academic performance, a 14% increase in workplace outcomes, and a 10% increase enjoyment boost for hopeful people.[80]

Just as an Army Pathfinder is trained to create and establish pathways for their team members, so it is for the credible hopeful leader. Without the Pathfinders' contribution to goal accomplishment, the mission is jeopardized. Pathfinders lead the way and their team members are depending upon them to do what they have been trained to do. Considering Lopez's research, hope repeatedly *"chooses the way, clears the way and confirms the way"* for goal accomplishment, both personally and organizationally.

When Pathfinders deploy ahead of their units, it is not an option to find a path for their team members—it must be done. Creating and establishing hope organizationally is not an option—it must be done. The terrain or assignments within the organization may be challenging and difficult but a Pathfinder must choose the way.

Choosing the way means to look for the path of least resistance or problems that can hinder the team's goal accomplishment. *Clearing the way* may also include reading in between the lines. Pay attention to what your co-workers or team members say or don't

---

[80] Lopez, p.50-51.

say. It's usually the things that are being ignored organizationally that need the most attention.

Confirming the way is a matter of trust by knowing yourself and your team. It involves training and trusting your team members or employees to do their jobs, which consistently builds trust that undergirds and strengthens organizational hope. These are all means that further aids the credible leader to create and confirm the way of establishing a growth mindset and not a fixed mindset for both personal and organizational goal accomplishment.

None of Them Is Free of Obstacles

"The boy who is going to make a great man must not make up his mind merely to overcome a thousand obstacles, but to win in spite of a thousand repulses and defeats."

Theodore Roosevelt

As an example of this core element of hope, Lopez tells the story of John Fetterman, mayor of Braddock, Pennsylvania, who uses *"hope as a hammer."* Braddock like many industrial towns is an old steel town that had its glory days during Andrew Carnegie's steel empire of the early 20th century. Yet when Fetterman arrived in 2001, the town was nearly dead, having lost 90% of its population and 90% of its buildings.

With no community center or playground, for the kids of the town, Fetterman negotiated a publicity deal with Levi Jeans. The company set a national ad campaign in Braddock, utilized local townspeople, and most importantly, donated a $1 million community center that was named in honor of a slain child. With no grocery stores or restaurants, Braddock was a full desert.

Fetterman helped develop a 2-acre urban garden that provides programs for families and extra vegetables for sale in nearby towns. Fetterman has hope about the future of small-town America. His belief system includes the fact that *"A leader should give people more options. Creating as many different opportunities and allow people to define their success is crucial."* Lifelong resident of Braddock Jerry Cannon sums up Fetterman's efforts: *"He's one of the few people that gave us hope for the future. He gave us opportunities with jobs. He gave us a reason to wake up every day and a place to go."* [81]

Former President Theodore Roosevelt, became living proof that desire, determination, and dedication can overcome any and all obstacles and keep hope alive. In early childhood Roosevelt overcame violent attacks of bronchial asthma that felt as though he were suffocating in his sleep. These attacks left him a weak and awkward child. In addition to the asthma, he was severely nearsighted child that was not discovered until he was 13.

As he grew older Roosevelt turned to games and sports that called for strength, endurance, and

---

[81] Lopez, 185-185.

skill, such as boxing, wrestling, obstacle riding, and mountain climbing as a means to cope with his awkwardness and humiliation.

A young Theodore married Alice Lee, who died four years after their marriage from unknown puerperal complications following the birth of their daughter Alice.

His mother died of typhoid fever only 12 hours after his wife's death. The 26-year-old Roosevelt was left alone to raise his young baby by himself.

One day as he was boxing with a young captain, his opponent forgot to pull his punches and hit Roosevelt's left eye. The blow caused a hemorrhage, followed by a detachment of the retina and almost total blindness.

On October 14, 1912, in Milwaukee, John Shrank shot Roosevelt in the chest with a .38 Colt revolver as he stood there waving at the crowd and he continued on with his scheduled speech that lasted approximately 50 minutes."[82] This amended version of the life of our former President is an incredible example of overcoming obstacles. The determination to succeed at any and every endeavor of his life kept hope alive for the duration of his life and leadership.

Throughout history, the repeated theme of keeping hope alive is seen as a necessary component of the human reality. On October 29, 1941, to the boys at Harrow School, Winston Churchill said, *"Never, never,*

---

[82] http://www.healthguidance.org/entry/8931/1/The-Health-Of-The-President-Theodore-Roosevelt.html. Accessed March 31, 2015.

in nothing great or small, large or petty, never give in except to convictions of honor and good sense. Never yield to force; never yield to the apparently overwhelming might of the enemy."[83] The world was as turbulent and uncertain for Roosevelt and Churchill in their era as it is for us now.

What remains a constant bright light in dark times is the existence and sustaining of hope. Sustaining hope when confronted with adversity becomes the counteragent for obstacles and setbacks. It is the credible leader that develops and possess the capability to restore people's hope in the future. Team members and employees, although it may not be verbalized, want to follow leaders that maintain a positive, confident, can-do approach in business and in life. By this type of leadership example, they help to sustain hope.[84]

Sustaining Hope

The credible leaders have the responsibility to keep hope alive organizationally. They must strengthen the beliefs of those that they serve, and that any struggles that they are called upon to deal with will produce a more promising future. Without the pressure that is

---

[83] http://www.winstonchurchill.org/resources/quotations/quotes-faq. Accessed March 31, 2015.
[84] Kouzes, James and Posner, Barry. Credibility: How Leaders Gain and Lose It Why People Demand It. (San Francisco: Jossey-Bass), 2011, p. 153.

applied to a lump of coal, the diamond that is on the inside will never be produced.

Keeping hope alive enables one to endure the pressure that on occasion appears to be too difficult to withstand. The only antidote to the increased cynicism and stresses of these times is renewed faith in our human capacity to believe. It is an intensely optimistic belief that together leaders and team members can overcome the difficulties of today and tomorrow.[85] Credible leaders sustain hope by painting positive images of the future and they neither hide nor are immune to the challenges of the day. Even when things go wrong within the organization, credible leaders bounce back by taking charge of the situation. They keep hope alive when they recognize the dedication of others to pursue excellence, especially when the struggle is difficult and challenging.[86]

Norman Cousins adds additional insight to this concept from his book *Headfirst: The Biology of Hope*. In his experience, Cousins observed that when some cancer patients were presented with a serious diagnosis, that many responded with a fierce determination to overcome. He went on to say that these patients did not deny the diagnosis. They chose to deny *the verdict* that is usually associated with it.[87]

When confronted with life-threatening diseases, or failing businesses, or a marriage that is in trouble,

---

[85] IBID, 154.
[86] IBID, 155.
[87] IBID, 157.

credible leaders must listen to the diagnosis, they must listen to the reality, and they must *"take hold of hope"* in cases of adversity.

From this perspective, credible leaders accept the diagnosis, but they do not accept defeat and do not become consumed by self-pity and grief. By taking hold of hope they *regroup, reassess,* and *resolutely* move forward.[88]

None of us will be able to escape the challenges that life brings. The evening news or a casual review of the Internet reminds us of the condition of the world in which we live. Yet in the midst of all of the bad news, the credible leader *"keeps hope alive."* How do you keep hope alive? How is this accomplished? It is by the *"recruitment of hope."* [89] To recruit is to enlist or enroll, to renew and restore. When people struggle or feel overwhelmed by what they are currently experiencing there are two questions that may be asked to help them reconnect with the ability to be their own agent of change and restorer of hope.

The first question that may be asked is, *"Who makes you feel like you matter?"* This may be a friend, a teacher, a relative. A person in your past or present life who made you feel understood, valued, and encouraged.

The second question is, *"What really matters to you?"* This question is designed to remind the person of what is important and what they have to offer the

---

[88] IBID, 158.
[89] Lopez, Shane. Making Hope Happen: Create the Future You Want For Yourself and Others. (New York: Atria Books) 2013, p. 105.

world. Examples such as, it *matters* that I love my family. It *matters* that I want to make a difference in my community. It *matters* that I enjoy helping people. It *matters* that I'm a good father and mother. It *matters* that I help my children and grandchildren to succeed in their chosen life endeavors. To recall what matters most to you is to enroll and renew the influence of hope as an agent of change. It is a reconnecting with one's identity and purpose that makes a difference in the world in which we live simply because they matter.

Someone once said *"Change is inevitable; progress is optional."* A person does not have to change, but change is occurring whether we like to change or agree with change. Progress is simply another way to say that I am moving forward. Moving forward, in this instance, is by a credible, practiced hope. It is the credible leader (hopeful leader) that trains to live and believe as John Gardner believed that through *"hope we can finally find our way through to a better world."* Leaders past and present have the responsibility to *"pay it forward,"* by passing the principle and baton of credibility to future leaders. The most essential quality for leadership is not *perfection* but *credibility*.

Credibility is the competent leader's currency that, if invested well in people, will strengthen their personal trust account within the organization. If people trust you, they will follow you. How do you build credibility? Not by pretending to be perfect, but by *being honest*. All of which establishes and solidifies organizationally a confidence that cultivates hope for the future.

SUMMATION: CREDIBILITY—THE KEY TO ORGANIZATIONAL EFFECTIVENESS

Credibility is simply the quality of being believable or worthy of trust. The root of the word *"credibility"* is *"credo,"* which means *"I believe"* in its original Latin root.[90] Credibility is the feeling of trust and respect that a leader inspires in others that is believable. It is this type of credibility and believability that is the key to team member's confidence in the organization to which they belong.

A path to this type of credibility includes the seven mindsets of professionalism. A professional is someone who is qualified and certified, normally after a particular course of study or years of preparation in a particular occupation as proficient or knowledgeable.

The seven mindsets of professionalism are as follows:

1. *Professionals Have a Bias for Results.*
2. *Professionals Realize (and Act Like) They're Part of Something Bigger than Themselves.*
3. *Professionals Know Things Get Better When They Get Better.*
4. *Professionals Have Personal Standards That Often Transcend Organizational Ones.*

---

[90] http://www.etymonline.com. Accessed March 21, 2015.

5. *Professionals Know Personal Integrity Is All They Have.*
6. *Professionals Aspire to Be Masters of Their Emotions, Not Enslaved by Them.*
7. *Professionals Aspire to Reveal Value in Others*

Becoming qualified in these seven mindsets has the potential and ability to further concretize organizational believability and credibility. In these seven mindsets, there is an amalgamation of people and organizational goals that accentuates a genuine asylum or place of refuge both for employees and the organization. These seven mindsets further transcend temperament, social hierarchy, and intellectual prowess because they are principle centered or true in any context or environment.

Establishing or building the credibility of interpersonal relationships means that leaders must connect with team members or employees where they are. The competent leader has to take the time to set up and sustain relationships. If you wait for others to establish relationships with you first, you may spend a lot of time waiting!

The credible competent leader creates a path to building relationships by being a *R.A.T.* The attributes of a *R.A.T.* are:

- *R*-espected/Reliable
- *A*-ccountable/Ardent
- *T*-enacious/Tailored

People trust what they believe to be real and authentic. This is birthed from the truth of a morality that is unmoved by the status quo. Authentic leaders genuinely desire to serve others through their leadership. They are more interested in empowering the people they lead to make a difference than they are in power, money, or prestige for themselves. Trust and authenticity empowers a cultivation of hope for the future organizationally.

Psychologist Shane Lopez says that hope can be learned and hopeful people share four core beliefs:

- The future will be better than the present.
- I have the power to make it so.
- There are many paths to my goals.
- None of them is free of obstacles.

As a person of hope, although everything may not be as positive as I may desire, I believe that the future will be better. I believe this because my leaders and the organization to which I belong make continual deposits into their *"account of credibility."*

History records that Winston Churchill took a steamship through German submarine-infested waters around Christmas in 1941, just after the Empire of Japan attacked Pearl Harbor, drawing the U.S. into World War II. Addressing the U.S. Congress Churchill stated, *"Sure I am that this day, now we are the masters of our fate; that the task which has been set us is not above our strength; that its pangs and toils are not beyond our endurance. As long as we have faith in our cause and an unconquerable will-power, salvation will not be denied us."*[91] An indomitable declaration of hope reflecting the mindset that together we have the ability to make it so by our own hands.

The competent leader is a master of his or her own fate as a model of credibility. Team members or employees will reach farther and dig deeper in their daily efforts if they believe in their leaders and the organization to which they belong. The key to organizational effectiveness that will *always* be the key is believability that gives me credibility as a competent leader with those that I lead.

---

[91] http://ghostsofdc.org/2012/03/14/the-masters-of-our-fate-winston-churchill-addresses-congress-1942/. Accessed March 31, 2015.

QUESTIONS FOR REFLECTION

. . . .

1. From your positon as a leader in your organization, what operational procedures appear to be eroding credibility and what recommendations would you make to senior leadership for improvement?

2. Identify any potential obstacles or roadblocks to question number 1 and create an action plan to overcome resistant concerning each obstacle identified for the betterment of the organization.

3. If you relate to people who are different than you with less passion than others, how do you increase or strengthen this necessary aspect of believability and credibility for the sake of the team and the organization?

4. John William Gardner, former Secretary of Health, Education, and Welfare under President Lyndon B. Johnson and founder of Common Cause, believed that through *hope we can finally find our way through to a better world.* As a competent leader how do you instill in members of your team that through hope we can find our way to a better organization and that the future will be better than the present in the face of constant failure, loss, disappointment, and discouragement?

5. You are the owner or CEO of an organization that you notice over the last few years has lost or is losing its nature of genuine professionalism. You notice this both from the *"daily attitudes"* of people who work for you and the feel that we have *"lost our edge"* as professionals. What do you do?

QUOTES OF PRINCIPLED LEADERS

"Change is inevitable; progress is optional." Anonymous
"Credibility is a leader's currency. With it, he or she is solvent. Without it, they are bankrupt."

John Maxwell

"Your reputation and integrity are everything. Follow through on what you say you are going to do. Your credibility can only be built over time and it is built from the history of your words and actions."

Maria Razumich

"To be persuasive, we must be believable; to be believable, we must be credible; to be credible, we must be truthful."

Edward R. Murrow

"Build your credibility so you won't have to the same thing twice before someone believes it."

Unknown

"Be humble, you could be wrong."

Unknown

SESSION IV

INTENTIONALITY IN ORGANIZATIONAL OPERATION AND ADMINISTRATION

Foundation

"A true leader has the confidence to stand alone, the courage to make tough decisions, and compassion to listen to the needs of others. He does not set out to be a leader, but becomes one by the quality of his actions and the integrity of his intent."

Douglas McArthur

To be intentional is to do something on purpose or deliberately, that which is done in a specified or planned manner. When we consider the term *operation* for the purposes of this session, it means *"a process of a practical form of work or production."* It can also mean the *"exertion of force, power or influence."*

Administration is a compound word comprised of two words: *"ad+minister."* To be a minister means one who serves. In its original Latin root, the word minister means aid, help, and cooperation. Therefore, an intentional leader *adds ministry (serves), aid, help, and cooperation* to the organization or community to which he or she belongs.

At the individual level, the intentional leader focuses on individual team members' actions, habits, or competencies. The focus organizationally are the same three elements of actions, habits, and competencies. Operationally, these same elements are the desired state of leaders at every level.

Ensuring the sustainability of the desired state individually and organizationally becomes the intentional leader's responsibility. It is possible that over a period of time that actions, habits, and competencies can decline or drift into a less desired state. The intentional leader recognizes that the desired state requires a consistent investment of energy for the purpose of sustainability. Intentionality also requires the aid of others that includes help and cooperation among team members in the organization. When executed in a planned, specified manner, intentionality becomes a catalyst that creates a championship mentality that endures. [92]

It has been said that honesty is the best policy. Actually, honesty is the *only* policy! The ability to

[92] http://www.case.edu/provost/ideal/doc/
Boyatzis_2006_intentional_change.pdf. Accessed May 21, 2015.

assess and be honest with self and the organization to which the intentional leader belongs is critical to the right or proper administration of the organization's operation. Answering the question, *"Are my (and the organizations) actions, habits and competencies in line with the stated and publicized values and goals?"* To say one thing and to do another in any organization creates an attitude of disbelief or cynicism amongst employees or team members.

This consequently erodes a team member's desire to give a 100% effort daily towards accomplishing expressed organizational goals and values when the organization is not doing the same. The culture, or work environment, if cultivated intentionally, will dramatically improve an organization's ability to execute. In other words, people will perform and give 100% effort to the organization because they want to.

Intentional culture development is transformative with consistent strategies for self-sustaining, positive work environments. This type of culture engages the hearts and minds of team members or employees to the point that they are committed to the vision, direction, and values of the organization and are inspired to do their best work. These are all signs of a healthy culture within the organization. An unhealthy culture can create an unhealthy work environment that creates an:

- Inability to attract and retain quality people
- People not working together

- Apathy and lack of enthusiasm for the organization
- Lack of initiative, accountability and responsibility

The intentional leader consistently and strategically ensures that the health (aid, help) and well-being of the organization (cooperation) is in place and functioning.

A Formula One race car and a Ford Fiesta are both cars, but they are created, sustained, and maintained for different purposes.

A race car is designed for speed for the purpose of winning a race. A Ford Fiesta is a family car designed for basic transportation for a family. Both cars do what they were designed and created to do. The intentional leader understands their purpose in the organization is to lead. This type of leader also ensures that their team members fulfill their unique, distinct purpose. One team member maybe a *"Formula One Race Car,"* and another team member maybe a *"Ford Fiesta,"* but they are both vital to the operation and administration.

The intentional leader becomes a skilled *"operational* (influential) *leader,"* capable of combining the unique, distinct members of the organization and fueling individual purpose with dedication and devotion to succeed. When you possess a desire (passion) to do or to be something…*"if it comes from without you won't be there long. When it comes from within you will be there forever."*

It is an intrinsic intention unmoved by external distractions. Not moved by outward rewards or accolades, but rather by the intrinsic satisfaction that you are in the world to make a difference. This is the daily determination; this is the daily dedication of the intentional leader that makes a difference.

PART I: THE 4 C'S OF OPERATIONAL INTENTIONALITY

When we consider a portion of the definition of *operation* in the foundation of this session, which can mean the *"exertion of force, power or influence,"* there are at least two key components necessary for intentionality. First, it is imperative that the intentional leader develops his or her own philosophy of operation. Second, a pattern or model is needed to facilitate the operation. This portion of the session offers the model or pattern of *"context, creating your story, conversation, and culture"* as a means of operational intentionality.

Context

"For me context is the key—from that comes the understanding of everything."

Kenneth Noland

The quote above from artist Kenneth Noland is rooted in art history. Robert Belton states, *"as complex as works of art typically are there are three general categories about the elements of art; form, content or context."*[93] Context can refer to a historical time, physical setting, and/or a particular social setting. Although there are three elements or categories of art history, Noland's

---

[93] fccs.ok.ubc.ca/about/links/resources/arthistory/elements.html. Accessed Junes 6, 2015.

perspective is that context provides *"the understanding of everything."*

The dictionary defines context as, *"the situation in which something happens. The group of conditions that exist where and when something happens."*[94] Context further helps to explain the meaning of a thing.

If we agree or buy into the definitions of Noland and what the dictionary states to us, context then becomes a pillar of organizational operation.

Every individual member of the organization or team brings a particular context along with them to the work place environment. If we were raised in an affirming environment that particular context has most likely shaped our mindset positively. The converse is also true. If most of a person's work experience has been in a context that is negative, the likelihood of that employee possessing a negative attitude is heightened. In other words, context can sometimes be good and sometimes it can be bad.

Perhaps the greatest asset in creating and shaping an organizational context that will produce the greatest results at any time and any place is active listening. Active listening involves intentional engagement with the person or parties involved in the communication. In the context of the organizational environment, the ability to listen is essential for the right conditions for comprehension and understanding. In a conversation,

---

94 http://www.merriam-webster.com/dictionary/context. Accessed June 4, 2015.

many are listening for the purpose of responding (getting their point across) and not comprehending.

As soon as this type of leader has a "reply" in mind, they stop listening and wait to reply. Positional leaders or the *"I'm in charge"* type of leader oftentimes speak from this preceding place or posture of leadership. Margaret Thatcher once stated, *"Being powerful is like being a lady. If you have to tell people you are, you aren't."*[95] If a leader has to tell people that they are in charge, the conditions or context of that relationship have been harmed and their leadership influence has been hindered. Intentional leaders speak from a place of comprehension and understanding of the context prior to speaking because they have practiced active listening. In this dynamic, the intentional leader has to contend and navigate through both the *external* context of the organization and the *internal* context of the individual team member. The organization's external context is much easier to understand simply because of the established standards, rules, and guidelines. The internal (sometimes emotional) context that employees or team members possess is not so easy. As a lifelong learner, the intentional leader makes time for periodic evaluation of the conditions or context in which he or she leads. Context is intermingled with every interaction that we have.

Therefore, the intentional leader learns how to ask the right questions of the organization and those that they lead because *context matters* to the individual and it matters to the organization. The intentional leader therefore must have a mindset and develop the ability to create and shape the context that will produce the greatest results. Capabilities, standards, relationships, and guidelines are all a part of the organizational context that has been created. Although a good organizational context may be in place, the question is, can the context become better? The answer to this question may be discovered through a *"context of collaboration"* in our evaluation of the organization as intentional leaders.

Bill Bowerman and Phil Knight are the co-founders of shoe and apparel giant Nike. However, it was neither Bowerman nor Knight's idea to name the company Nike. The company was originally founded as Blue Ribbon Sports in 1964. It was in Bowerman's and Knight's *collaboration* with their first employee Jeff Johnson who suggested the name Nike, and the rest is a part of the organization's history.[96] Collaboration is simply a working together for a goal or purpose. It is in the context of collaboration with their first team member or employee that the organization certainly became better.

According to Forbes.com, Nike is the most valuable sports brand in the world, worth $15.9 billion (excluding its autonomous brands like Cole Haan, Converse, Umbro, and Hurley), an increase of

---

[96] www.businessinsider.com/history-of-nike-facts-about-its-50th-anniversary. Accessed June 7, 2015.

$1.4 billion, or 9.7%, since Forbes first Fab 40 in 2007. That means the Nike name accounts for over one-third of the athletic gear maker's market value.[97] Nike in the original Greek is translated means *"victory."* Every time a new employee becomes a part of the team and they hear or say the name Nike, they are reminded that victory is rooted in the operation of this organization. Nelson Farris, Nike's director of corporate education, says that Nike is about *"people getting things done. All of the corporate ups and downs, winning companies hold onto their values. To survive the downs, you have to understand that teamwork is keeping promises, and keeping commitments."* [98]

Each new team member who is hired is called "Ekin." Ekin is simply Nike spelled backwards. Ekins undergo a nine-day rookie camp at Nike headquarters in Beaverton, Oregon. Dave Pearson, a training manager at Nike, says that, *"the aim of the camp is in essence to connect Ekins today back to Nike's foundation and heritage. If we connect people to that, chances are that they won't view Nike as just another place to work."*[99]

From its beginning stages in 1964 as Blue Ribbon Sports, Nike has created a very powerful model for establishing the conditions and context for leaders and team members that aims to connect both the

[97] http://www.forbes.com/sites/mikeozanian/2014/10/07/the-forbes-fab-40-the-worlds-most-valuable-sports-brands-2014/. Accessed June 11, 2015.
[98] http://www.fastcompany.com/38979/nike-story-just-tell-it. Accessed June 11, 2015.
[99] IBID.

past and the future for victory as an organization. The intentional leader creates a story or context of leadership that team members like Nike's Ekins will want to read because of the proven path of success or victory that is visible and tangible.

As you write the story that *you* want people to read, ensure that is written by your character and make it a best-seller, intentionally.

Creating Your Story

What I've learned about writing from many gifted authors is that many times the original manuscript or the story must be rewritten over and over and over again. As a lifelong learner, the intentional leader many times must learn some lessons over and over and over again. The redundancy or repetitive learning is necessary to become *"skilled at writing"* one's leadership story. To create or write a story of intentional leadership that others will desire to read, the lessons in the leader's life's story need to be *"revised, refined and ready* to be read by the public.

Revised

To revise is to *"reconsider and alter (something) in the light of further evidence"* or discovery. The writing center at the University of North Carolina says that revision literally means to *"see again,"* to look at something from a fresh, critical perspective. It is an ongoing process of rethinking.[100] This is the intentional leader's place of self-evaluation.

Consider the elements of your leadership story such as balance and clarity. Balance means even or equal amounts of direction and instruction with encouragement and inspiration. Clarity means that the reader (team member) *"gets"* what the leader is communicating by example and deed. The leadership example matches the direction and instruction. Professional and relational consistently without pretense or arrogance. A pretentious and arrogant leader will discover sooner or later, that although now in a position of leadership, no one is actually following.

However, a balance of encouragement and inspiration with direction and instruction creates the kind of work environment that is both pleasurable and productive for the organization and employees. Revision assists the intentional leader to constantly evaluate the readability of their story. Revision, which includes honest self-evaluation, answers the question for the leader, Is my story worth reading?

Refined

To revise is to evaluate the readability or content whereas when you refine something, you make it

---

[100] http://writingcenter.unc.edu/handouts/revising-drafts/. Accessed June 16, 2015.

better. Refining something *"requires fixing its flaws."*[101] Although sometimes difficult to acknowledge for some, this is the place of addressing and refining character flaws. Ralph Waldo Emerson once stated, *"Our strength grows out of our weakness."* Where there are virtues, there are also vices. A vice simply implies shortcomings or imperfections in the leader. Secrecy is the enemy to addressing our individual weaknesses. No matter what our status or position in life, the need for refinement will always be necessary. Our weaknesses are part of being human. Honest self-evaluation many times carries the intentional leader to the place of accountability with another.

Accountability simply means that I have the ability to count for something. This is the place where the intentional leader allows a trusted mentor or peer to help identify specific areas of moral weakness for the purpose of growing in accountability to defeat any and all character flaws. Character flaws cannot be denied. If a leader attempts to deny the reality of our weaknesses, there is coming a point where we will all be confronted with our "own iceberg."

History has argued that it was not the iceberg that sank the Titanic, but the flawed rivets that held the steel plates together. [102] Whatever a leader is made of, be it education, experience, tenacity, integrity,

---

[101] http://www.vocabulary.com/dictionary/refine. Accessed June 16, 2015.
[102] http://www.usnews.com/news/national/articles/2008/09/25/the-secret-of-how-the-titanic-sunk. Accessed June 16, 2015.

truthfulness, or fidelity, there is always a need for refining.

There are many books that are available with titles such as *Ten Steps to Success* or *How to Succeed in Life*. I am certainly not being critical of books with themes such as these. However, there are very few books on the market today with a thesis that addresses the fact that all it takes is *one* vice, or all it takes is *one* moment of moral weakness, to lose or destroy a 20- or 30-year career. In the wake of such destruction oftentimes families are also destroyed because of *one* vice or *one* moment of immorality.

Accountability is a vital aspect of the refining process that helps to write a story of success through the landmines of our weaknesses and vices by building upon virtues and strength of character that lasts a lifetime. This is a chapter that must be written in every intentional leader's story.

Ready

The manuscript of the leader's life at this point has gone through the process of *revision*, the process of *refinement*, and now the leader's story is *ready* to be "*read*" by the public.

While attending a workshop at Central Texas College, Killeen, Texas, in the summer of 2015, I discovered a young leader's story worth reading. In the parking lot of the college, I noticed a young lady picking up trash in the area of the student center.

She didn't appear to be part of the maintenance or janitorial staff and when I asked her why she was picking up trash and she replied that, *"she felt that it was her responsibility."* I'm not sure if she understood this or not, but I had the opportunity to *"read a portion of the story"* that this young lady was writing about her life. The responsibility that this young lady (she was 19) had acquired was motivation enough for her to become an unknown and unpaid member of the maintenance or janitorial staff of the college. I believe that it is safe to say that this young lady did not enroll at Central Texas College for the purpose of being a member of the maintenance staff. As a student, she had responsibilities to study, go to class, and other "student stuff." Yet as an emerging leader, she was making a difference across the campus of Central Texas College by the story of her leadership influence being written by the example of her life.

The lesson that I learned from this 19-year-old student that day is that as she was picking up trash, her motivation for what she was doing was for *others'* sake and not necessarily her own. This young student believed in and possessed an internal motivation that became her self-imposed assignment or responsibility of picking up trash at her college. This internal motivation or drive will undoubtedly encourage and influence others as she continues to write her leadership story. She encouraged and influenced me on that day by being a trash collector, which too many would see as insignificant, but in actuality, was a great thing to witness from this young leader.

Vincent Van Gogh once stated, *"Great things are done by a series of small things brought together."* Intentional leaders recognize and realize that everyday another chapter of their story is being written by their actions, that sometimes may seem to be small and insignificant but produces a considerable return on the investment made.

An adaptation of a poem by one unknown author summarizes this portion of the session succinctly. *"You are writing a story. A chapter each day by deeds that you do, by words that you say. People read what you write, whether faithless or true, what becomes your life's story is up to you."*[103]

Conversation

Our traditional understanding of the word *conversation* carries the idea of a dialogue or exchange of information between two or more people or parties. Our focus on conversation in this portion of the session carries a different meaning. *The Online Etymology Dictionary* states that the word *conversation* carries the connotation of *"living together, having dealings with others."* It can also mean a *"manner of conducting oneself in the world."* This meaning derives from the Latin *"conversationem"* which means, *"the act of living with"* or literally *"turnabout with."*[104]

---

[103] http://bethanyipc.sg/poems/bulletin071021.htm. Accessed June 11, 2015.
[104] http://www.etymonline.com/. Accessed June 4, 2015.

As a manner of conducting oneself in the world (our workplace), or to *turnabout* with other team members on a daily basis requires several factors in operation for organizational cooperation. These factors are *humility, diversity, harmony, and unity.*

Humility

"The X-factor of great leadership is not personality, it is humility."

Jim Collins

The term *humility* is not utilized in many organizational settings because of how it is seen or viewed.

The most likely reason is that from this perspective humility is seen as being a negative, soft or weak trait and not necessary for leaders.

When viewed from a positive perspective, humility or humbleness is a quality of being courteously respectful of others. It is the opposite of *aggressiveness, arrogance, boastfulness, and vanity.*[105] When considered in this context, humility is actually strength under control or a virtue that builds strength of character. The dictionary defines humility as the *"quality or state of not thinking you are better than other people."* Additionally, a leader who operates with the attribute of humility is capable of recognizing and admitting

---

[105] http://www.christianbiblereference.org/humility.htm. Accessed June 20, 2015.

one's weaknesses. This admission doesn't necessarily need to occur publicly, but it must occur to *"the person in the mirror."* Practiced humility provides a security that enables a leader to seek help and guidance from others. It is asking the very difficult question of a trusted friend or mentor, *"What weaknesses do you see in me as a leader?"* These type of questions can *only* be asked of trusted mentors and friends.

Denying our shortcomings after receiving feedback from trusted mentors, friends, and advisors is a sign of ego and will restrict personal and professional development. An egocentric leader is headed down the road of frustration due to eventual alienation from the team and organization. No one desires to follow someone that leads and operates narcissistically. There is little room for ego, arrogance or narcissism in truly great leadership. To develop as a leader requires one to learn from mistakes and deal with adversity.

To do this requires admitting fallibility, which is an act of humility. It creates an open and inspiring environment where creativity is welcomed and encouraged. This will lead to a more productive and positive atmosphere.

Diversity

"Diversity may be the hardest thing for a society to live with, and perhaps the most dangerous thing for a society to be without."

William Sloane Coffin Jr.

In today's society, European-American, Asian-American, Irish-American, African American, etc., are all very familiar terms of identifying various groups of people. These terms are all born of social constructs or ideology. These distinct terms highlight our distinctive ethnicity; however, what is sometimes overlooked in these descriptions are what we have in common besides the American.

What we all have, regardless of our social-economic description or status as human beings, is that we are all human. This is the idea and mindset of diversity from the perspective of the intentional leader or the simple fact that we are better together.

In April 2010, the University of North Carolina at Chapel Hill School of Public Health conducted a survey of students and asked the question, *"How would you define diversity?"*[106] As you would imagine, there was quite a diversity of responses from within this body of approximately 29,000 students. A quick perusal of the study validates to an extent the strength of diversity. The basic root of the word diversity is from the Latin *"diversus"* meaning *"different in character or quality."*[107] The students at the University of North Carolina provided a wide array of thoughts behind what diversity actually is. The intentional leader understands this wide array of how people think about diversity and uses it to the advantage of the

---

[106] http://www.sph.unc.edu/files/2013/07/define_diversity.pdf. Accessed June 21, 2015.
[107] http://www.etymonline.com/. Accessed June 21, 2015.

organization. Some see diversity as a weakness while the intentional leaders view is that diversity is a strength.

Diversity conversations have a tendency to discuss *"social mores"* (ethnicity, culture, religion, etc.) without the equally important mores of inclusion and acceptance. What this means for the intentional leader is a respect for others right to be different while not disrespecting the values and mores of the organization and other team members. Disruption of the values of the organization and other team members because of personal desires or beliefs should never conflict with the standard and values of the organization.

Any type of behavior or conduct because of diversity by a team member that is contrary to organizational values must be swiftly quarantined and eradicated. Everyone has a right to be diverse, but no one has a right to undermine or obstruct organizational standards because of diversity.

Wherever there is *"diseased behavior"* (contrary to organizational values), there will be *"dis-ease"* among team members. The intentional leader discovers the source, eradicates the source, and *"vaccinates"* the organization as a preventative measure. The vaccination is a reiteration as often as needed, that we are all different, but what makes us a community are the values, mission, reputation, and identity of the organization.

Every team member and leader is expected to understand and abide by the rules of foundation, values, and standards of the organization. From the moment that a person becomes a part of the organization, that person is accepted as they are and contrary behavior to organizational norms is unacceptable and may be grounds for dismissal from the team. The varied viewpoints represented by a sample of students from the UNC helps to make this point. Words and statements like openness, bringing together, immersion, integration, heterogeneity, culture, and experiences are all expressed in the definitions above that reminds us of our wide array of thought in our society concerning diversity.

The intentional leader as a lifelong learner takes a diversified team that is different in character and quality and makes that team a unit or makes them one with the organization by inclusion and acceptance. Respecting our diversity, being open to learn from one another, and combining our distinctive experiences can become our strength. Strength through diversity has the potential to produce organizational harmony.

Harmony

"We live in a world of discord and we can either participate in its chaos or seek to be agents of harmony and good will."
Anonymous

Harmony for the purposes of this session is defined as *"a relationship in which various components exist together without destroying one another. It is further characterized by a lack of conflict or by agreement."*[108] Synonyms for harmony include accord, concord, cooperation like-mindedness, and unanimity.

Most are familiar with the concept of four-part harmony in the realm of music. In the original Greek, the root word of harmony is translated as *"harmos."*

Which means *"a joining"* as in the connection of joints in the body.[109] According to HealthPages.org, there are approximately 400 joints in the human body.

These joints allow both *movement* and *flexibility.* Most body joints allow us to move, and some only allow movement in certain ways. Fixed or immovable joints allow no movement. [110] Following the analogy of joints in the human body, harmony within the organization allows for both *movement* and *flexibility.*

There is an old proverb that says *"blessed are the flexible for they shall not be bent out of shape."* Depending upon the size of one's organization, untold multitudes of moving parts (joints) are needed to accomplish the mission. Each department and every person in that department has a role in the multitude of moving parts. In other words, as a joint they are connected to other joints for accomplishing the task at hand.

On December 1, 1913, Henry Ford began the operation of his assembly line for his Model T Ford.

---

[108] http://www.thefreedictionary.com/harmony. Accessed June 23, 2015.
[109] Vines, William Edwy. Vines Expository Dictionary of Old and New Testament Words [Internet]. Copyright 1940 [Cited June 23, 2015]. Available from: http://studybible.info/vines/.
[110] http://www.healthpages.org/anatomy-function/musculoskeletal-system-bones-joints-cartilage-ligaments/. Accessed June 23, 2015.

Each person on that assembly line was responsible for a role (joint) in producing that particular Model T Ford.

Ford had been trying to increase his factories' productivity for years. The workers who built his Model A, which later became the Model N cars (the Model T's predecessors), arranged the parts in a row on the floor, put the various parts of the Model T on skids and dragged them down the line as they worked, which had proven to not be very efficient in assembling the automobiles.

To increase productivity, Ford broke the Model T's assembly into 84 discrete steps and trained each of his workers (joints) to be responsible for one portion of the assembly. In order to lower the price of his cars, Ford figured, he would just have to find a way to build them more efficiently and the assembly line was the answer.[111]

Each worker in harmony with the others understood their particular role as a joint in the organization and because of Ford's innovation, the modern-day assembly line is in place and functioning in organizations virtually all around the globe. Where there is harmony, each joint connected to the next joint is equally valued in the process of accomplishing the organizations task or assignment. For those that have become *"fixed or immovable joints that allow no movement,"* the intentional leader underscores to

[111] http://www.history.com/this-day-in-history/fords-assembly-line-starts-rolling. Accessed June 23, 2015.

each team member, individually and collectively, the importance of movement that creates momentum.

Where there is a dislocation of joints (team members) characterized by conflict or lack of agreement, the intentional leader diagnoses the issue and writes a prescription (problem-solving) that restores health to that portion of the organization. Due to Henry Ford's innovative response to increasing the production of his Model T, an affordable car for all, by June 4, 1924, the 10-millionth Model T came off of his assembly line.[112]

This never could have been accomplished without every joint, every team member of Ford Motor Company being in harmony with one another. Harmony always has the potential of creating authentic unity. This is the heartbeat of conversation, living together, having dealings with others.

Unity

"We are only as strong as we are united, as weak as we are divided."

J. K. Rowling

Unity is defined as, *"being in harmony or one in spirit. A unified group or body."* Unity is also defined as, *"constancy, continuity, or fixity of purpose."*[113] In many traditional wedding ceremonies one portion of the

---

[112] IBID. Accessed June 23, 2015.

[113] http://www.yourdictionary.com/unity. Accessed June 26, 2015.

service is the lighting of the unity candle. The unity candle is a single candle that the bride and the groom light simultaneously symbolizing the union or joining of the two that have become one.

The actualization of unity is symbolized with a bride and groom when both operate in a basic principle attributed to St. Francis of Assisi. *"Seek first to understand then to be understood."* Although the bride and groom obviously love one another to the point where the intention is to live as husband and wife for the rest of their lives, now that they are married, they must *learn how to stay married!*

This is where again the concept of *personal* or people-oriented leadership as opposed to simply *positional* leadership tips the scales of purposeful relationships in favor of the leader and organization. It is important to note that union is not always necessarily unity. You can tie the tail of a cat and dog together and you will have a union, but you can be certain that there is no unity!

In other words, what this means is that we can be together in an organization (same team) and not be together. In any relationship, there will be disagreements or tension. From this principle attributed to St. Francis, it is the intentional leader focused on unity within the organization who *"seeks first to understand then to be understood."*

There are four basic steps that will assist the intentional leader in seeking first to understand the tension or disagreement then to understand how to go and grow as an organization beyond the tension or problem:

- Confrontation of the tension (problem)
- Consolidation of the facts
- Collaboration for the answers
- Celebration of the resolution

Wherever you have people working together, you have the potential for misunderstandings. You cannot ignore the tension or disagreements because they have the potential to spill over into the organizational atmosphere. For the intentional leader to *confront* the tension is simply to recognize that there is a problem that must be addressed.

Consolidation of all the facts of the disagreement or tension provides the intentional leader with the elements or the cause. *Collaboration* for the answers must include all team members who were involved. Most people will support that which they have helped to create. When all parties have been heard and recommendations have been placed on the proverbial table, now the intentional leader can make an *informed* decision instead of an *emotional* decision.

The intentional leader ensures that the collaborative effort removes emotions from the equation and places all team members on equal ground in the move towards resolution. An intentional leader makes every person feel valued and important. No member of the team feels as if another has a favored position in the organization.

In the collaborative effort, the emphasis is on not *who* is right, but rather *what's* right for the individuals involved and the organization.

Whatever amount of time is needed in this collaborative effort, it must be invested because working through the problem or tension together is another tremendous means of building the team.

Everyone's input is valued (and they know it) and now is the time of *celebration* of the resolution. Albert Einstein once stated, *"in the middle of difficulty lies opportunity."* Resolution provides an opportunity for building relationships capable of enduring the difficulties.

With the principle of being a lifelong learner in the forefront, an opportunity for learning is in the middle of any and all difficulties. The intentional leader (and team members) focused on unity discover together the solution that may not always be in the policies and procedures manual. Although we may *disagree*, we do not have to be *disagreeable* in our *disagreeing*. We can agree to disagree, but it will not and cannot affect the operation and administration of the organization! What matters the most is that the organizations mission does not suffer or compromised because someone may disagree with another on the team.

As it was with the cat and the dog whose tails were tied together, the aim is unity and not just union! If there is a team member who consistently and constantly causes tension and problems, the question that may need to be asked is, *"Do you still want to be a part of this team?"* If the answer is no… then it's time to let that team member go. If the answer is yes, the intentional leader invests and mentors that team member to success. There may have been some undisclosed personal problems for this team member that no one is aware of.

It is impossible to be in unity (whole) with others when an individual is not whole with one's self. The answer or resolution is not always a particular problem-solving matrix. Sometimes, it is simply about connecting at the heart of the tension and the heart of the people involved.

An anonymous writer said, *"Speak in such a way that others want to listen to you. Listen in such a way that others want to speak to you."* Connecting at the heart of the problem and the heart of people involved includes *confrontation, consolidation, collaboration* and ultimately *celebration*. The intentional leader communicates in such a manner that people want to *listen* and *speak* to this leader who connects. It is leadership of this nature that possesses the capability to re-connect all that were involved in tense or difficult interpersonal circumstances back to harmony with the aim of organizational unity and the fact that we are better together.

Culture

"Our background (culture) and circumstances may have influenced who we are, but we are responsible for who we become."

James Rhineheart

The word *culture* from its original Latin root, *"cultura,"* means *"a cultivating."* In its figurative sense, it is a *"cultivation through education,"* *the intellectual side of civilization"* and that of *"collective customs and achievements of a people."*[114] Geert Hofstede, Gert Jan Hofstede, and Michael Minkov in their book, *Cultures and Organizations, Software of the Mind* state, *"Every person carries within him or herself patterns of thinking, feeling, and potential ways to act that have been learned throughout that person's lifetime."*

According to the authors, culture consists of the collective *programming of the mind* or how a person thinks that distinguishes the members of one group or category of people from others. Within this definition, the authors state that culture is learned and is not innate.[115] Understanding this framework, the intentional leader creates within the culture of the organization a learning environment of acceptance and belonging where everyone *believes* that we are

---

[114] http://www.etymonline.com/. Accessed June 30, 2015.
[115] Geert Hofstede, Gert Jan Hofstede and Michael Minkov. Cultures and Organizations: Software of The Mind. (New York, McGraw-Hill) 2010, p. 5-6.

all a part of the same culture (team) that becomes the incentive for how we think, feel and act.

In our conversation (lifestyle) of *having dealings with others*, or our *manner of conducting oneself* (working) with co-workers, there is a valued component of the Army culture that is called the *"battle buddy."* The concept or principle of the battle buddy is wherever you go, your battle buddy is there with you.

Responsibility and accountability are embedded in this principle of the battle buddy. If there was an appointment or training session that you needed to get to, oftentimes your battle buddy was responsible and accountable to ensure you made it to the appointed place. If your Drill Sergeant found you without your battle buddy, severe consequences were headed your way! The *"battle buddy"* is a distinct and unique part of the Army culture. Responsibility for completing tasks, conditions, and assignments still belonged to the individual soldier.

Yet the concept or principle of the battle buddy also included the necessity of relationship and encouragement.

Fort Knox Kentucky was once the home of the United States Army and Armor Center (now located at Fort Benning, Georgia). A part of completing basic training at Fort Knox was a 5-mile, 8-mile, and 12-mile road march that was a test of a soldier's physical endurance. As I recall during my days of basic training in 1976 at Fort Knox, the 5-mile road march was nicknamed *"misery,"* the 8-mile road march was nicknamed *"heartbreak,"* and the 12-mile road march was nicknamed *"agony."*

These road marches were so nicknamed due to the extremely difficult hills and terrain that were a part of each one. Each soldier had to carry his or her own approximately 60 pounds of gear. The 12-mile road march was at the beginning of the final week of basic training.

If a soldier did not complete the 12-mile road march in the allotted time of 3 hours, he or she would not be able to graduate with the rest of the class.

As my company of approximately 100 soldiers was completing our final leg of the 12-mile road march we reached the top of the hill and the finish line was in sight! We had more than 30 minutes to spare. We were tired and yet elated because we could see the finish line right before us. We were within just a few hundred yards of being able to drop our 60 pounds of gear after marching up and down hills of various elevations and degrees.

Agony was almost over! Yet when some of us reached the top of the hill with the finish line in sight, our Drill Sergeant stopped us and told us to look back down Agony's last hill. Many of the soldiers in our company appeared as if they were not going to make this last very steeply inclined hill. Our Drill Sergeant made those of us who were within a few hundred yards of the finish line *go back down to the bottom of the hill* and help those who didn't look like they were going to make it to the top. The principal or concept of the battle buddy was in full operation.

What our Drill Sergeant was teaching us that day, although everybody was exhausted and tired after hours of road marching, what really needed to be conquered was the fact that *no one is left behind.*

No matter how difficult the task or the assignment may be, we encourage one another, we are better together, and we will all make it to the finish line together.

Approaching daily tasks and assignments from this perspective creates a *"cultivation through education,"* where we consistently and continually learn how to work through any difficulties or challenges and we do it together. The intentional leader deposits this ideal of being a *battle buddy* to someone in the customs and culture of the organization. Meaning I am responsible and I am accountable to not only myself, but to my *battle buddy* and to the organization to which I belong.

The intentional leader determines to create a culture within the organization that no matter how exhausted or tired we may be, no matter what difficulties we confront as an organization, we are better together.

PART II: CREATING INTENTIONAL MOMENTUM THROUGH S.T.A.R. LEADERS

Normally when we think of personalities as stars, we think of exceptionally gifted sports figures, Hollywood actors, or famous entertainers. This is not the case with becoming an intentional *S.T.A.R.* leader.

A *S.T.A.R.* leader is one who focuses his or her attention and intentions upon a particular *strategy* that is aimed at *transformation* by *affirmation* that produces desired *results* within the organization.

- *S*-trategy
- *T*-ransformation
- *A*-ffirmation
- *R*-esults

Within this *S.T.A.R.* pattern is also the idea of momentum. J. C. Larreche states, *"Momentum is a phenomenon by which under specific conditions accumulates energy from its own success and provides ever increasing acceleration for organizations that harness it and build on it."*

Larreche further believes that momentum cannot be ordered into existence; momentum must become *"conscious procedure."*[116] The conscious procedure

---

[116] Larreche, J.C. The Momentum Effect: How To Ignite Exceptional Growth. (Upper Saddle River: Wharton School Publishing), 2008, p. xxi, 228.

suggested in this portion of the session is an intentional *S.T.A.R.* pattern.

Strategy

Strategy is defined as *"the art and science of planning and marshalling resources for their most efficient and effective use."*[117] Strategy is a plan or a means of getting from here to there.

Strategy is purposeful action over a period of time. The term is derived from the Greek word for generalship or leading an army. With this basic definition, strategy therefore involves focus and choice in creating organizational momentum. Although there are tremendous amounts of research and data that focus on business strategy (product, increased revenue, etc.) or military strategy (basic tactics of warfare), the intent of this portion of the session is to feature the people behind strategies.

To marshal or assemble an organization's resources begins with a focus on people. Whatever the organizational structure or entity may be, any strategy must begin with people or members of the team.

Modern-day technology is certainly a great ally to accomplishing goals and objectives. However, the greatest resource that any organization has will always be its employees or team members who operate the technology. The intentional leader must look at and

[117] http://www.businessdictionary.com/definition/strategy.html. Accessed June 14, 2015.

evaluate the most efficient means of *"people power"* because it is people who power the organization.

It is also important to note that, although the goals and objectives of the organization have been verbalized at staff meetings and reiterated in an employee manual, this many times is insufficient in creating organizational momentum. There is a science to creating momentum. Science may be defined as *"facts or principles gained by systematic study gained through observation."*

A *S.T.A.R.* leader focuses on a *"systematic study"* of the organization and team members in order to gain knowledge (of people) and it is always a matter of choice and intentionality. Developing the ability to ask the right questions while studying or researching will most likely provide the right answers. Good questions challenge the leaders' thinking and helps to reshape and stimulate solutions that create momentum.

In *Life Without Principle,* Henry David Thoreau stated, *"The greatest compliment was paid to me today. Someone asked me what I thought and actually attended to my answer."*[118]

Asking a team member, the simple question *"What do you think?"* provides the *S.T.A.R.* leader with at least two positive results that help to create momentum:

- Amazement from team member
- Internal satisfaction from the team member

---

[118] http://www.evancarmichael.com/Business-Coach/223/The-Power-of-Asking-People-What-They-Think--AND-then-Really-Listening-and-Hearing-What-They-Say.html. Accessed June 14, 2015.

Amazement from the team member in the sense that senior leadership thought enough of them as a member of the team to answer! Internal satisfaction for the team member in the sense of a contribution that has the potential to be adopted by the organization.

Internal satisfaction in knowing that if what a team member has to contribute is not considered to be valuable, no one would ask. This will create momentum.

No two people are alike and no two organizations are alike and therefore the *S.T.A.R.* leader astutely observes and learns from the *"outside in."* Learning people from interactions such as the preceding creates a vantage point that assists the process of *"balance and congruence."* Any organization that is out of balance is destined for problem after problem. To create momentum, a balance of rules, guidelines, and regulations and organizational health is necessary. Rules are to maintain order and facilitate operations and administration. However, if the work environment is like a prison camp, retention of quality team members is going to be difficult. It is always easier going downhill then going up a hill. One way to keep momentum going is to constantly have greater goals.

Celebrate small victories that contribute to bigger victories or achievements. The *S.T.A.R.* leader intentionally establishes within the organization an appreciation for work completed and the accomplishment of today's goals, without losing focus on tomorrow.

Sports teams are quite familiar with the reality of a shift in momentum. Whether it is steal and a slam dunk during a basketball game or an interception by the opposing football team that is taken in for a touchdown, momentum can and will help a team win the game. *S.T.A.R.* leaders recognize that if you don't go after what you want, you will never have it. If you don't step (move) forward, you always be in the same place.

Albert Einstein once said, *"Life is like riding a bicycle. To keep your balance, you must keep moving."* Momentum always requires movement and *S.T.A.R.* leaders ask the right questions that facilitate and create momentum that keeps the organization balanced, congruent, and moving forward.

Transformation

"First comes thought; then organization of that thought, into ideas and plans; then transformation (change) of those plans into reality. The beginning, as you will observe, is in your imagination."

Napoleon Hill

Transformation in an organizational context is *"a process of profound and radical change that orients an organization in a new direction and takes it to an entirely different level of effectiveness. Transformation further implies a basic change of character and little or no resemblance with the past configuration or structure."*[119]

A transformational perspective is often needed in an organization due to the reality of *adversity* that may be accompanied by an undercurrent of *amorality*. An *amoral* person is one who has no moral standards, restraints, or principles and an indifference to questions of right or wrong. For the *amoral* person, it simply doesn't matter as long as the circumstances do not affect him.

Dr. Martin Luther King Jr. once stated ***"Our lives begin to end the day we become silent about things that matter."*** An *immoral* person knows what society (the organization) considers right and wrong, yet makes the choice to do wrong anyway. In adversity, a *S.T.A.R.* leader focuses on developing the capability of transforming adverse circumstances (amoral or immoral) or influences that could impact the entire team or organization. This type of leader is not birthed overnight. While some are born with an aptitude for leadership, intentional *S.T.A.R.* leaders are *made.*

Through training, experience, honest self-evaluation, and self-reflection, they think about *transformation* of self and others by learning how to work with different personalities and adverse negative influences. They learn to nurture, motivate, and inspire. In the *"school of hard knocks,"* negative, adverse influences (adversity) are confronted, which is the

---

[119] http://www.businessdictionary.com/definition/transformation.html. Accessed June 14, 2015.

genesis of a *"personal or organizational metamorphosis."* The means of accomplishing a metamorphosis of either type is by establishing or **re-establishing** an *"organizational morality"* or an effective operational sense of right and wrong.

Organizational Morality

Establishing or re-establishing an organizational metamorphosis begins with *never, absolutely never, compromising the principles, standards, and values of the organization.* Consistency and constancy provide stability of operation.

You cannot go to Burger King and expect to order a Big Mac. A Big Mac is not a part of Burger King's values and standards. Neither can you go to McDonald's and expect to order a Whopper. A Whopper is inconsistent with McDonald's organizational structure and values. In other words, it would be wrong (immoral) to expect McDonald's to have the Whopper on the menu and equally wrong (immoral) for Burger King to have the Big Mac on the menu! This would be a compromise of the principles, standards and values of their respective organizations.

When there is *compromise,* there is also the potential for *confusion.* Who are we and what makes us who we are as an organization is foundational for consistency, constancy, and stability. An understanding of the organization's nature and identity helps to combat adversity and negative influences.

Championship teams rally around the positive and not the negative even in adversity. Many times in the locker rooms of our sports teams, sometimes the players want to meet *without the coaches* because of some adverse situations.

When the values (winning) and standards of the organization are constant and consistent, *"the players"* (employees) know what is expected and recognize when and where something has gone wrong and it is time for a team meeting. This is transformational leadership that has learned how to win through adversity.

Negative influences (laissez-faire, amoral) or attitudes on the team are not tolerated; the team as a whole focused on success will speak up. For championship-caliber teams, any player who has brought too much negative attention or influence to the team will, many times, face the other players and they will handle this issue. If there are people who still insist on compromising the morals and standards of organization, it's probably time to change the people around you. This cannot be ignored or neglected. To win the championship for the organization that maybe experiencing adversity, each member of the team must have the heart and mindset of a champion and refuse to allow adversity or difficulties to undermine the goals and standards of the team (organization).

What this means as transformational leaders is that as a team we each rise to an entirely different level of effectiveness because we have made the choice to *NEVER, NEVER, ABSOLUTELY NEVER, COMPROMISE OUR VALUES AND STANDARDS.*

A Personal and Organizational Metamorphosis

Metamorphosis maybe defined as, *"the process or result of changing from one appearance, state, or phase to another. A complete change of circumstances, character or nature."*[120]

From the preceding definition we can therefore state that an organizational metamorphosis is the actualization of a change of character.

Adelphia Communications Corporation was ranked as the fifth-largest cable company in the U.S. before it yielded to bankruptcy in 2002 due to internal corruption. The company incurred $2.3 billion debt and its founders were charged with securities violations. The senior leadership of the company created a complicated cash-management system where they diverted funds to other family-owned entities for their own financial gain.[121]

The Enron scandal revealed in October 2001 proved to us what a company and its leadership are capable of when they are obsessed with making money with little or no concern for the people of the company.

---

[120] http://www.thefreedictionary.com/metamorphosis. Accessed July 4, 2015.

[121] http://list25.com/25-biggest-corporate-scandals-ever/. Accessed July 4, 2015.

The company had incurred tremendous financial losses as a result of arrogance, greed, and foolishness from the top tier of leadership to its lowest level of leadership. [122]At some point, the organization's standards and values began to corrode and nothing was done until it was too late to restore a sense of right and wrong. Enron will remain in our minds for years to come, as a classic example of the corruption and corrosion of organizational morality.

Corruption is a fact and reality of the world in which we live because of a lack of morality. Corruption can be defined as *"the use of a position of trust or power for dishonest gain."*

It is further defined as *"wrongdoing on the part of those in authority through means that are illegitimate, immoral, or incompatible with ethical standards."*[123] Corrosion maybe defined as *"a gradual wearing away of something; to impair or deteriorate."* Edmund Burke once stated, *"All that is necessary for evil to triumph is for good men to do nothing."*[124]

The examples of companies like Adelphia Communications and Enron are vivid reminders of the corruption and corrosion of organizational morality where perhaps *"good men did nothing"* until it was too late. Many times the corruption and corrosion of morality is cloaked or clothed in professionalism

---

[122] http://www.investopedia.com/articles/stocks/09/enron-collapse.asp. Accessed July 4, 2015.

[123] www.dictionary.com. Accessed July 4, 2015.

[124] http://www.constitution.org/cons/quotes01.htm. Accessed July 4, 2015.

and charisma. Most professionals in this day and age are not *impressed* by charisma or professional scripted rhetoric.

A *S.T.A.R.* leader does not seek or desire to be *impressive*. However, because of the humility of their character, they leave an *impression* of authenticity in their footsteps. It bears repeating that a *S.T.A.R.* leader (intentionally) focuses on *strategy, transformation, affirmation, and results.*

In other words, the *S.T.A.R.* leader employs a *strategy* for *transformation* of any corruptive or corrosive behavior by personal and organizational *affirmation* that creates positive *results*. Standing upon the standards of the organization provides the foundation for the *S.T.A.R.* leader to recognize potential corruptive or corrosive behavior in any shape or form. Strategies include:

- Examining the ethical climate often.
- Making a public commitment to being an ethical organization.
- Keeping the lines of communication open at every level. Creating a safe, confidential reporting system for unethical conduct or behavior.
- Establishing and empowering an internal or external ethics committee to which *everyone is accountable.*

Being *awake, alert,* and *aware* to the potential of corruptive or corrosive behavior is an intentional strategy for daily operation for the *S.T.A.R.* leader. This also means paying attention to the *"little things that if ignored can become big things."* If a leader or member of the team is constantly late or consistently making excuses for missing deadlines, this is an example of *"a little thing that can become a big thing."*

The standards of the organization are in the process of corrosion, and it is evident a personal metamorphosis is most likely needed.

In addition to this, any leader who portrays an attitude of *"just do what I say"* is in need of a personal metamorphosis.

A complete change of the circumstances, character and nature of Adelphia Communications Corporation was needed, but it never occurred until it was too late.

A complete change of the circumstances, character and nature of Enron was needed much earlier than October 2001, and because there was no change in the organization's nature or character, the end result was destruction by implosion.

A *personal* metamorphosis (change is constant) sometimes is the beginning of a renewed *organizational* metamorphosis (what needs to change).

A clear sense of morality or that which is right or wrong established or re-established, both personally and organizationally, provides a safeguard against corrosion of values and standards that potentially leads to corruption and destruction.

A *S.T.A.R* leader is *awake, alert,* and *aware* of the *"little things that can become big things"* and is strategically prepared to be a transformational leader in adversity amid the reality of a laissez-faire, amoral society.

This is the mindset and position of an intentional leader, one that makes a difference.

Affirmation

A basic definition of *affirmation* is *"a positive statement."* Synonyms for affirmation include, certification, confirmation and approval. During a recent study, 200,000 employees were interviewed to discover what was missing in their respective organizations' levels of productivity.

The study concluded that *appreciation* and *affirmation* were at the top of the list as to what employees wanted most from their leaders. The research implies that receiving affirmation is a basic human need. [125] In its original Latin etymology, the word *affirmation* means *"to make steady, strengthen, steadfast and unwavering."*[126] In essence it is the influence (leadership) of the words that we speak to another that strengthens, or makes another steady and unwavering.

Forty-nine years ago Robert F. Kennedy delivered his famous *"Day of Affirmation"* speech at the University of Capetown, Capetown, South Africa, on June 6, 1966, to 18,000 school officials and students who had gathered in spite of bitter cold and wind.

---

[125] http://odb.org/2013/09/10/the-power-of-affirmation/. Accessed July 5, 2015.
[126] http://www.etymonline.com/index-firm. Accessed July 5, 2015.

Apartheid was still very much alive and well in South Africa and by his presence Robert Kennedy was determined to make a difference. At one point of his speech, Kennedy stated, *"at the heart of freedom and democracy is the belief that the individual man, the child of God, is the touchstone of value, and all society, all groups and states exist for that person's benefit."*[127]

Another very salient point that Kennedy made in his speech is *"the essential humanity of man can be protected and preserved only where government must answer — not just to the wealthy, not just to those of a particular religion, not just to those of a particular race, but to all people."*[128]

In his speech in South Africa that lasted approximately 34 minutes, Robert F. Kennedy made an intentional effort *"to make steady, strengthen and create a steadfast and unwavering"* hope in the future in a nation that like many others struggled with equality. Although some would consider Kennedy's speech only from a political perspective, his words carried the strength of affirmation to over 18,000 people who were present on that day.

The point here is that it does not matter if it was 49 years ago, or 49 minutes ago, the influence (leadership) of affirmation can create steadfast, unwavering, and unmovable hope, trust, and commitment within an organization. There are those that would prefer to

[127] http://www.huffingtonpost.com/kerry-kennedy/day-of-affirmation-ripple_b_1576014.html. Accessed July 5, 2015.
[128] IBID.

work in isolation or away from others; as apartheid suggested. Equality in this era in South Africa was indeed a privilege and not a right of all human beings. Yet sociologists tell us that human beings were not created to live or work in isolation from one another.

What a person may prefer is one thing, but productivity is another thing organizationally as suggested by the earlier interview of 200,000 employees. As an employee or member of an organization, intrinsic cooperation with others and every member of the team must be important and affirmed. The *S.T.A.R.* leader operating from the position or principles of Kennedy's speech to 18,000 school officials and students during the height of apartheid is intentional not only about *transformation* (the way we think) but also *affirmation* (the way we speak) to others. Affirmation cultivates acceptance and acceptance is the foundation of trust.

In other words, a positive statement, the power and influence of our words (affirmation), can encourage and further solidify solidarity between the leader and the led. If in fact the study of 200,000 employees mentioned earlier implies that affirmation is a basic human need, this would also imply that *we must have it* (affirmation) to survive.

The *S.T.A.R.* leader, as did Robert Kennedy, understands that affirmation must not simply be noted and celebrated as a *"Day of Affirmation"* but rather daily. In so doing, we are assisting other team members and leaders to survive the negative, destructive forces of our world. A positive statement, the power and influence of the words that we speak to others, is capable of strengthening and creating steady unwavering hope and trust as a reality organizationally.

John F. Kennedy, Robert F. Kennedy, Martin Luther King, Mother Theresa, and countless *S.T.A.R.* transformational leaders like them influenced the world by this principle of affirmation. As Robert Kennedy stated 49 years ago, *"we exist for another person's benefit"* and affirmation is beneficial for all. Leaders such as the aforementioned, transform and affirm others because of the single and fundamental reason: it is the right thing to do.

Results

After all of the *strategic* planning, the intention to *transform*, and the purposeful *affirmation*, the question remains that at the end of the proverbial day: What are the results? *Merriam Webster's Dictionary* says that a result is *"that which happened because of something else that happened or was done before, to be caused by something else."* The Urban Dictionary says that results relate to *"a form of corporate strategy focused on outcomes and achievements."*

Synonyms are conclusion, outcome, development, determination, and end. *S.T.A.R.* leaders are results oriented because of *intentional* strategy, transformation and affirmation.

How does the *S.T.A.R.* leader who is oriented on results obtain the desired results? The answer is to create an organizational mindset of professionalism.

Professionals are trustworthy, competent, and respectful, act with integrity, and are considerate and empathetic. By affirming and upholding traits like these and others is a means of creating professionalism in the organization. No matter what my role or responsibility maybe, the ideal is to convince and persuade every employee or team member that *"I am a professional."*

A professional is one that has been trained and possesses certain certifiable skills in a particular job or occupation (profession). A professional has acquired the tools and skills necessary to do the job, and always performs to the highest standards and abilities of their trade. Professionalism is associated with the mastery of one's given trade or expertise. Creating and maintaining a mindset of professionalism creates a *results-oriented, trusted* professional that is a *"co-owner"* of the organization.

A team member or employee who as a professional approaches daily assignments as a *"co-owner,"* also takes responsibility and ownership for increased productivity (and success) of the organization. It is a partnership with their leadership that provides results such as:

- Improved performance
- More employee participation and involvement

- Increased feelings of competency
- Increased employee commitment to the work
- More creativity and innovation
- Higher employee morale and satisfaction with work

Author Steven Pressfield stated, *"The difference between an amateur and a professional is in their habits. An amateur has amateur habits. A professional has professional habits. We can never free ourselves from habit. But we can replace bad habits with good ones."* This is the mindset of a professional that produces results. Professionalism or being a professional is not always about a business suit and tie. Being a professional is to also take pride in one's occupation. From this perspective, it is as Martin Luther King stated, *"If it falls to your lot to be a street sweeper, sweep streets like Michelangelo painted pictures, sweep streets like Beethoven composed music. Sweep streets like Shakespeare wrote poetry. Sweep streets so well that all the host of heaven and earth will have to pause and say: Here lived a great street sweeper who swept his job well."* [129]

Beginning with self, the *S.T.A.R.* leader becomes the personification of professionalism set by the example of Dr. King's *"street sweeper"* who personified professional pride in job performance. Creating the mindset of habitual professionalism as a standard is a high ideal. Yet it is always the challenge of the *S.T.A.R.*

---

[129] http://www.beliefnet.com/Quotes/Inspiration/M/Martin-Luther-King-Jr/If-A-Man-Is-Called-To-Be-A-Streetsweeper. Accessed July 14, 2015.

leader to never lower the standards or expectations of professional conduct, but rather to always bring team members or employees up to the standards of professionalism.

It is the *S.T.A.R.* leaders' purposeful, intentional *strategic* objective that *transforms* the ordinary into the extraordinary through *affirmation* that accomplishes this *result* and refuses to allow the standards of professionalism to be compromised.

PART III: DEFINING MOMENTS DEFINE INTENTIONAL ORGANIZATIONS

The *Oxford Cambridge Dictionary* says that a defining moment is, *"the point at which a situation is clearly seen to start to change."* Freedictionary.com says that a defining moment is, *"a point at which the essential nature or character of a person, or group is revealed or identified."* Yourdictionary.com says that a defining moment is, *"a moment in time that defines something, such as a person's success or failure achievement or demise."*

Each of the three preceding viewpoints or definitions of defining moments provide some understanding of what defines intentional organizations. Each of the three contribute an intricate element of defining moments. *Change, character*, and *time* are these three principles.

Someone once said that *"change is inevitable, yet progress is optional."* For those that do not recognize that *change* affects the *character* or nature of the organization, then it is simply a matter of *time* before the operation and administration begin to corrode. These three principles, *"change, character, and time,"* are in constant motion and operation and never take sick leave or are late for work.

The intentional leader and organization recognize how to utilize these principles to their advantage. Intentional leaders are ordinary people who did extraordinary things because circumstances made demands on their potential. The intentional leader presses forward daily to develop the ability to inspire, and this becomes the place of *"mobilization of the troops,"* or a defining moment that occurs through purposeful relationships.

There are those in some leadership circles who would insist upon the power of *"positional leadership"* as opposed to a more *"personal"* approach to leadership. Positional leadership is rooted primarily in *power* and *authority,* while personal leadership is rooted primarily in the *person* and *affirmation.*

It is not an either or perspective, it is both. If positional leadership is utilized solely, then there will be very little hope for establishing positive relationships with those that they lead. Positional leadership does not include the more personal components of relationship or teambuilding.

Yet when the position is balanced with a personal perspective for connecting with employees or team members the organization becomes the benefactor of this approach to intentional leadership. Anyone can be appointed to a position by hard work and a personal desire to succeed.

However, when it comes to the nature of leadership which is influence, the same attributes of hard work and a personal desire to succeed will not necessarily make that person an effective leader. To lead from one's position neglects many of the human aspects of leading others. Without *"relationship there is no authentic leadership."*

Relating to me on *"my ship"* involves purposeful relationship building. For the intentional leader, it means discovering what each team member's personal aspirations and career goals may be. Leadership—of any kind, in any location, for any purpose—is about working with people. [130]

Out of these relationships, intentional leaders are not afraid to establish strong friendships because they are secure in their abilities and purpose. You cannot really help or lead people if you do not like people. The intentional leader has discovered truly who they are and the authority under which they function.

The principles of effective operation and administration implicitly provides us with the necessity of understanding the power of relationships in achieving organizational goals. It is by *affirmation* and not *isolation* that the bonds of organizational achievement is strengthened and solidified.

The story was once told of a Roman emperor who sought to discover humanity's original language thinking that it might be Hebrew, Greek, or Latin. So this particular emperor experimented by isolating a few infants. The nurse that was involved with these infants was sworn to absolute silence in the presence of the children and no one ever spoke to her in the

---

[130] http://www.bloomberg.com/bw/stories/2007-07-12/position-leaders-destined-to-disappointbusinessweek-business-news-stock-market-and-financial-advice. Accessed June 25, 2015.

presence of the infants. These infants never heard a single word or sound from a human voice. Tragically, within several months, these isolated infants died. A lamentable result of a bizarre search for knowledge gone awry. The emperor never learned the original language of humankind, but he did prove one thing: *"people cannot survive without relationships."*[131]

In essence what this story teaches us is that a philosophy such as this one of unknown Roman emperor is that any organization that operates in insolation without affirmation most likely will not survive.

We were not created to operate in isolation; we were created to live, work, and play in and through the influence of relationships that matter.

In these relationships that matter, leaders and team members alike experience the influence of affirmation that become defining moments within the organization. The intentional leader understands why they have been appointed to lead, and that understanding is the motivation for cultivating operational and administrative relationships within the organization that matter.

Every intentional leader and every team member brings unique talents and gifts to the table in the operation and administration of the organization's goals and objectives. James Kouzes and Barry Posner provide additional insight to the secret of achieving

---

[131] Morgan, Robert J. Stories and Illustrations. (Nashville: 2000), p.70.

these goals and objectives within the organization. In an interview entitled, *"The Secret to Success in Life"* by Kouzes and Posner discuss the impact of relationships in leadership for the intentional leader.

John Stanford is a retired major general, U.S. Army, former county manager of Fulton County Georgia, and superintendent of Seattle Public Schools. When Kouzes and Posner asked John Stanford the question how he would develop leaders, whether in college, in the military, in government, or in business, the following was his reply:

> *"In essence the secret to success in life is to **stay in love**. Staying in love gives you the fire to ignite other people, to see inside of other people, and to have a greater desire to get things done than other people. A person who is not loved doesn't really feel the kind of excitement that helps them to get ahead and lead others to achieve. I don't know any other fire, any other thing in life that is more exhilarating and is a more positive feeling than love."* [132]

Kouzes and Posner after researching leadership for over 30 years stated, *"Staying in love is not the answer we expected to get—at least not when we began our study of leadership. Through thousands of interviews and case analyses, we were constantly reminded of how many leaders*

---

[132] http://www.growthink.com/content/secret-success-business-and-life. Accessed April 19, 2015.

use the word love freely when talking about their own motivations to lead. At some point in his life and career, John Stanford walked into this epiphany or defining moment of his life and leadership." [133]

To be clear, a defining moment is *"a point at which the essential nature or character of a person, or group is revealed or identified."* A defining moment is also *"the point at which a situation is clearly seen to start to change, a moment in time that defines something, such as a person's success or failure, achievement or demise."* [134]

Staying in love with leading, with the people who do the work, are perpetual defining moments for the leader and the organization. I am a firm believer, *"we are today a result of the choices that we made yesterday."*

In the final analysis, intentional leadership is not an affair of the *head* (knowledge), intentional leadership is an affair of the *heart* (love).

From this vantage point as an intentional leader, love for others is not a secret. It is a character attribute that defines the intentional leaders for the rest of their lives and leadership.

The final component of this session looks briefly at six practices or strategies that, when applied, have the potential to aid in the operation and administration of the intentional leader and organization.

---

[133] IBID. Accessed April 19, 2015.
[134] http://www.yourdictionary.com/defining-moment. Accessed December 20, 2015.

PART IV: SIX PRACTICES OF AN INTENTIONAL LEADER

. . . .

The Practice of Approachability: This is creating the reality among those who follow you that as a leader you can be approached without fear. There is no aloofness or perception of *"don't bother me now, because I'm busy."*

It is practicing the giving of your undivided attention to the matter that has brought the team member or employee to your office. It is creating the reality that you can trusted as a responsible leader. Practicing and creating the perception of approachability means that those who follow a leader with this character trait are confident that no matter what the issue may be good or bad, they can approach the leader without fear.

The Practice of Immutability: Immutability carries the idea of not changing over time or unable to be changed. Not in the sense of rigidness or stubbornness. In this sense, immutability is a matter of the heart or a practice of character. It means that team members sense and know that as a responsible leader there are no *"chameleon tendencies"* that they have to be concerned about. Chameleons adapt to their surroundings in order to survive in a particular environment. A leader cannot operate as *Dr. Jekyll and Mr. Hyde*. Immutability is a practice of the heart that over a period of time creates a redundancy of

176

organizational expectations. This does not mean that change does not occur. Change is inevitable and constant. However, consistency and constancy of the leader's heart towards team members' well-being (immutability) provides stability that further produces a level of satisfaction and an *"extra-mile"* mentality that further creates momentum that moves team members and the organization forward.

The Practice of Accountability: Accountability means that as an intentional leader, you have the ability to count, to make a definitive difference. Accountability means that you accept responsibility for the outcomes expected of you—both good and bad. You don't blame others. And you don't blame the environment in which you work. There are always things you could have done—or *still can do*—to change the outcome.

The bottom line is that no organization can grow and prosper until the leaders are willing to step up and be answerable to not only the organization but also to those that they lead.

The Practice of Serviceability: A basic definition of serviceability carries the idea of *"to be ready fit, or able to be used."* In this sense, serviceability is both a matter of the heart (*character*) and of the hand (*capabilities*). The *Oxford English Dictionary* says that service is *"the act of helping or assisting."* The U.S. Army's fourth of seven values that soldiers are taught to adhere to is *"selfless service."* Selfless service is doing one's duty loyally without thought of recognition or gain. The basic building block of selfless service is the commitment to go a little further, endure a little longer, and look a little closer to see how the leader or team member can add to the effort of success for the organization. Selfless service leads to organizational teamwork that encompasses discipline, self-control and faith in the system.[135]

The practice of serviceability or selfless service reminds the intentional leader to be fit and *"ready to be used to help or assist others"* to accomplish tasks or any given assignments.

The Practice of Sustainability: To sustain is to *"strengthen or support physically or mentally."* [136] There are many avenues to the human heart. Sustainability is such an avenue. When followers or team members know that their leader is intent on sustaining their hopes and aspirations, loyalty, and commitment to the organization is concretized and effectuated. From this perspective, sustainability becomes the foundation upon which to build championship teams. Practicing a mindset of organizational sustainability through good and bad times further creates a culture of success and creates defining moments for intentional leaders to influence their organizations.

The Practice of Authority: When you look at any policeman, you already know that they are in a position of authority. When a policeman tells you do to something, most people are going to comply because

[135] http://www.army.mil/values/. Accessed April 12, 2015.
[136] www.oxfordenglishdictionary.com. Accessed April 12, 2015.

of the authority of the police officer's position. Most leaders are in a position of authority; what differs is how the authority is used. An authoritative positon of leadership for soldiers on the battlefield is essential. This is not the time for democracy or to take a vote on what must be done.

That is because with authority a person in the position of leadership is expected to take charge of any given situation. In other words, *"When in charge, be in charge!"* However, it is important to note that authority is not a dictatorship. If a leader chooses to use authority from this perspective, he or she has the potential to destroy credibility and trust.

Influence focuses on having an impact on someone's character, their development, or even the way they think to the point that people are ready to follow. Influence has the ability to direct or change the viewpoint or character of another that is grounded in credibility and trust.

A credible, competent, trusted leader understands the necessity of balancing authority and influence. There are certain circumstances where leading from authority or position is needed. There will be other times when leading from one's established influence is the better option. The intentional leader practices both and knows when one or the other is required.

A balanced approach of the preceding six practices consistently potentially establishes credibility and believability in the hearts and minds of employees and team members. When this pattern is perpetually espoused and practiced, the operation and administration of the organization can do nothing but succeed. In other words, the practice of this pattern has become intentional and everybody (leaders and team members) knows it and make the choice daily to live by this pattern.

SUMMATION: INTENTIONALITY IN ORGANIZATIONAL OPERATION AND ADMINISTRATION

To be intentional is to do something on purpose or deliberately—that which is done in a specified or planned manner.

When we consider the term *operation* for the purposes of this session, it means *"a process of a practical form of work or production."* It can also mean the *"exertion of force, power or influence."*

Administration is a compound word comprised of two words; *"ad+minister."* To be a minister means one that serves. In its original Latin root, the word *minister* means aid, help, and cooperation.

Therefore, an intentional leader *adds ministry (serves), aid, help, and cooperation* to the organization or community to which they belong. At the individual level, the intentional leader focuses on individual team members' actions, habits, or competencies. The focus organizationally are the same three elements actions, habits, or competencies. Operationally, these same elements are the desired state of leaders at every level. Ensuring the sustainability of the desired state individually and organizationally becomes the intentional leader's responsibility.

There are at least two key components necessary for intentionality. First, it is imperative that the intentional leader develops his or her own *philosophy of operation*. Second, a pattern or model is needed to facilitate the operation.

The model or pattern suggested in this session is that of *"context, creating your story, conversation, and culture"* as a means of operational intentionality.

The dictionary defines *context* as, *"the situation in which something happens. The group of conditions that exist where and when something happens.* It is not necessarily *situational* as much as it is *intentional,* or to grab hold of the conditions that provide meaning and understanding. As a lifelong learner, the intentional leader many times must learn some lessons over and over and over again.

To write or create one's leadership story that others will desire to read, the lessons in the leader's life story need to be *"revised, refined and ready* to be read by the public or by those in our organizations. For the purpose of this session, the *Online Etymology Dictionary* states that the word *conversation* carries the connotation of *"living together, having dealings with others."* It can also mean a *"manner of conducting oneself in the world."* This meaning derives from the Latin *"conversationem"* which means, *"the act of living with"* or literally *"turnabout with."*[137] Conversation can be defined as lifestyle or conduct. As a manner of conducting oneself in the world (our workplace), or to *"turnabout"* with other team members on a daily basis

---

[137] http://www.etymonline.com/. Accessed June 4, 2015.

requires several factors in operation for organizational cooperation. These factors are *"humility, diversity, harmony, and unity."*

Organizational culture begins with defining the word *culture*. The word from its original Latin root, *"cultura,"* means *"a cultivating."*

In its figurative sense, it is a *"cultivation through education," the intellectual side of civilization"* and that of *"collective customs and achievements of a people."* [138]

Geert Hofstede, Gert Jan Hofstede and Michael Minkov in their book, *Cultures and Organizations, Software of the Mind* state, *"Every person carries within him or herself patterns of thinking, feeling, and potential ways to act that have been learned throughout that person's lifetime."*[139]

Understanding this framework, the intentional leader creates within the culture of the organization to which they belong, a learning environment of acceptance and belonging where everyone *believes* that we are all a part of the same culture (team) that becomes the incentive for how we think, feel, and act. A *S.T.A.R.* leader intentionally creates and harnesses the power of momentum in their sphere of influence within the organization. J.C. Larreche states, *"Momentum is a phenomenon by which under specific conditions accumulates energy from its own success and*

---

[138] http://www.etymonline.com/. Accessed June 30, 2015.

[139] Geert Hofstede, Gert Jan Hofstede and Michael Minkov. Cultures and Organizations: Software of The Mind. (New York, McGraw-Hill) 2010, p. 5-6.

provides ever increasing acceleration for organizations that harness it and build on it."

Larreche further believes that momentum cannot be ordered into existence; momentum must become *"conscious procedure."*[140]

With the aid of Larreche's definition of momentum, a *S.T.A.R.* leader is one who creates organizational momentum with a particular *strategy* that is aimed at *transformation* and *affirmation* that produces desired *results* within the organization.

The *Oxford Cambridge Dictionary* says that a defining moment is, *"the point at which a situation is clearly seen to start to change."* Freedictionary.com says that a defining moment is, *"a point at which the essential nature or character of a person, or group is revealed or identified."* Yourdictionary.com says that a defining moment is, *"a moment in time that defines something, such as a person's success or failure achievement or demise."*

Each of the three preceding viewpoints or definitions of defining moments provide some understanding of what defines intentional organizations. Each of the three preceding definitions contribute an intricate element of defining moments. *Change, character,* and *time* are these three principles. Someone once said that *"change is inevitable, yet progress is optional."* For those who do not recognize that *change* affects the *character* or nature of the organization, then it is a matter of

---

[140] Larreche, J.C. The Momentum Effect: How To Ignite Exceptional Growth. (Upper Saddle River: Wharton School Publishing), 2008, p. xxi, 228.

time before the operation and administration begins to corrode.

These three principles, *"change, character, and time,"* are in constant motion and operation and never take sick leave or are late for work. The intentional leader and organization recognize how to utilize these principles to their advantage.

In order to sharpen and maintain their leadership edge, the intentional leaders practice their profession.

Six practices have been suggested for the intentional leader in this session: *"Approachability, immutability, accountability, serviceability, sustainability, and authority."*

A balanced approach of the preceding six practices consistently establishes relationship within one's leadership. When this pattern is perpetually espoused and practiced, the operation and administration of the organization can do nothing but succeed. In other words, the practice of this pattern has become a standard within the organization and everybody (leaders and team members) knows it and lives by this pattern intentionally.

QUESTIONS FOR REFLECTION

1. Context is defined as *"the group of conditions that exist where and when something happens that provides meaning and understanding."* What steps could you take to improve upon the context of your work environment?
2. How would you help a peer leader implement a *S.T.A.R.* pattern both personally and organizationally?
3. Reflect upon the most significant defining moment in your life. How has it informed and impacted your personal leadership philosophy?
4. Given the opportunity, how could you persuade members of your organization at every level (senior and junior) of the necessity of writing a personal leadership character story that is both believable and credible?
5. Using the overall principles in this session, what model would you construct for leading intentionally in your organization?

Quotes of Principled Leaders

....

"I believe the choice to be excellent begins with aligning your thoughts and words with the intention to require more from yourself."

Oprah Winfrey

"You are what you do, not what you say you'll do."

Anonymous

"Excellence is never an accident. It is the result of high intention, sincere effort, intelligent direction, skillful execution, and the vision to see obstacles as opportunities."

Anonymous

"The only person that you are destined to become is the person you decide (intend) to be."

Ralph Waldo Emerson

"Be concerned about your character and not your reputation, because your character is who you are and your reputation is only what people think you are."

Anonymous

"A wise man adapts himself to circumstances, as water shapes itself to the vessel that contains it."

Chinese Proverb

Notes